AMONG THE SO

A Goodly Heritage

AMONG THE SOVIET EVANGELICALS

A Goodly Heritage

Samuel J Nesdoly

THE BANNER OF TRUTH TRUST

THE BANNER OF TRUTH TRUST
3 Murrayfield Road, Edinburgh EH 12 6EL
PO Box 621, Carlisle, Pennsylvania 17013, USA

© *Samuel J Nesdoly 1986*
First published 1986
ISBN 0 85151 489 8

Set in 10½/12 Plantin at The Spartan Press Ltd
Lymington, Hants
Reproduced, printed and bound in Great Britain by
Hazell Watson & Viney Limited,
Member of the BPCC Group,
Aylesbury, Bucks

TO LIL,
MY GOD-GIVEN HELPMATE AND
SHARER OF THAT GOODLY
HERITAGE WHICH WE RE-DISCOVERED
TOGETHER

Contents

Illustrations

Foreword

Truly, as the writer of Ecclesiastes declares, "Of the making of many books there is no end". The story of the evangelicals in the Soviet Union has been told many times, most recently and most satisfactorily by Walter Sawatsky.[1] Why then yet another book on this subject?

Over the past few years I have spoken about the Soviet evangelicals on approximately one hundred occasions to university students, church groups, and service clubs in the United States and Canada. Despite the extensive literature and the massive, if selective, publicity by various organizations, the view of Soviet evangelicalism held even by these specially-interested listeners was often very simplistic, not to say distorted. In part, this was because of their reading patterns. Very few, unfortunately, were acquainted with the more balanced views of writers such as Sawatsky, Hans Brandenburg,[2] Michael Bourdeaux,[3] William Fletcher,[4] Steve Durasoff,[5] or even Peter and Anita Deyneka.[6] For all too many, a steady diet of sensationalist literature had convinced them that Soviet evangelicalism could be portrayed in a single, black-and-white snapshot. In reality, a better image is that of a three-dimensional, multi-media kaleidoscope.

Thus, there is room for a book on the Soviet evangelicals that endeavours to combine the scholarly qualities of balance, perspective, and a more comprehensive treatment with the popular writer's more personalized, human-interest/anecdotal approach. Of course, the richness and complexity of Soviet evangelicalism cannot be portrayed in a single book, even though it were much longer than this one. But the brief introduction and chronological survey provide at least some of the necessary historical background and sense of perspective. Though many aspects of the evangelical scene are discussed in this book, mine is certainly not a fully comprehensive treatment. Further, my assessments of church-state and inter-church relationships, along with comparative observations on Christianity in the USSR and North America, are not uncontroversial. Hopefully, however, thoughtful readers will discover enough factual information, insights, and well-supported conclusions to provide an accurate sketch-picture of the Soviet evangelicals. If this will stimulate them to investigate the subject more thoroughly, the first of my purposes in writing this book will have been fulfilled.

Whatever their problems and shortcomings, the persecuted Soviet evangelicals consistently demonstrate the kind of spiritual commitment, strength and joy that is at once an inspiration and a rebuke to comfortable North American Christians. Observing their day-to-day lives over a period of time gives one the uncanny impression of watching a re-enactment of the Book of Acts. As in the Near East in the first century, so in the contemporary USSR, Christ's true followers still suffer shame for His sake. And all the while they continue to live lives which show that they are indeed what their enemies mockingly call them – "Christians!" ("belonging to Christ").

The task of the preacher (and perhaps the Christian writer as well) is to comfort the afflicted and to stir up the comfortable. It is thus my earnest hope that some of my readers will be powerfully challenged by the stories of Anton and Vera, Philip, the dynamic young people, and a host of others. And if they should be moved to live lives of greater commitment, more vigorous witness, overflowing joy – *Slava Bogu*! (Glory to God!) – my second purpose will also have been fulfilled.

It will be clear from the tone of this book that my interest in the Soviet evangelicals is both personal and professional. As a writer of M.A. and Ph.D. theses on Russian Baptist history and as one who teaches university courses on the history of the USSR, I have endeavored to see Soviet evangelicalism in an overall context. As one who shares the faith of his paternal grandfather (a Russian Baptist preacher for over sixty years), I undoubtedly tend to see things as my fellow-evangelicals see them.

In 1971, during a brief visit to Leningrad, I was able to experience, for the first time, the thrill of direct discovery of my spiritual roots. Recollections of those experiences form part of the first two chapters of this book. Thanks to the Canada-USSR Academic Exchange Program, in 1978 my wife, Lil, and I were able to spend two months in the Soviet Union, visiting Leningrad, Moscow, Kiev, and our grandparents' home village of Borodianka in the Ukraine. Free from the limitations imposed by official commitments and escorted tours, both of us fairly fluent in the Russian language, we were thus able to speak freely and frankly with many Soviet citizens, both believers and unbelievers. In addition, we took the opportunity to attend twenty-eight services in eight different churches – six Union, one which belongs to the Reformers' Union of Churches, and one Independent.

As we talked and listened, observed and tried to co-ordinate our impressions, our somewhat abstract and general knowledge was enriched and deepened through exposure to the concrete and specific. And as we became more intimately acquainted with the complexities of Russian Baptism, we also came to a more profound appreciation of our goodly heritage. If this book can convey something of our sense of the nature and significance of that heritage, then my third purpose will also be fulfilled.

With few exceptions, the experiences described occurred in the order in which they appear in the book. Thanks to extensive note-taking, the use of *two* memories of many incidents – and a cassette tape recorder – conversations, though edited, have been reported almost verbatim. Unless otherwise indicated, the incidents were either personally observed by Lil and/or myself or reported to us by individuals in the USSR or Canada. Also, the characters are real, rather than fictitious, though their names (except for those of the pastors and some of our relatives) have been changed.

Two final explanatory comments should be added. Ukrainian nationalists might object to the "Russian-ness" of my descriptions of Kiev and Borodianka, but I have tried simply to report things as we saw and heard them. Similarly, non-Baptists might object to my use of the term Soviet Baptism as being essentially the same as Soviet evangelicalism. The latter term is certainly the more comprehensive, including, for example the Mennonites, Pentecostals, some Lutherans, as well as those essentially Baptist believers who prefer the name Evangelical Christians. But this last group, together with the Baptists proper, do, after all, make up the great majority of Soviet evangelicals. Furthermore, the term "Baptist" is commonly used by the public in the USSR to refer to the evangelicals in general.

1 W. Sawatsky, *Soviet Evangelicals since World War II* (1981)
2 Hans Brandenburg, *The Meek and the Mighty* (1976)
3 M. Bourdeaux, *Religious Ferment in Russia* (1968) also the journal *Religion in Communist Lands*

4 W. Fletcher and A. Strover, eds. *Religion and the Search for New Ideals in the USSR* (1967)
5 S. Durasoff, *The Russian Protestants* (1969)
6 A. and P. Deyneka *A Song in Siberia* (1978)

Introduction

A. EVANGELICALS IN THE USSR: AN OVERVIEW

In the course of its approximately century-long history the Baptist movement in the USSR has changed in shape while remaining essentially the same in substance. The scattered little groups of believers in the 1860s and 1870s have grown into a nation-wide community numbering, according to some estimates, close to three million. Once predominantly rural, Baptists have responded effectively to the general process of urbanization. Their thousands of little country congregations have been increasingly balanced by individual urban churches such as those in Talinn (Estonia), Leningrad, and Moscow with three to five thousand members each. Despite recurrent experiences of discrimination and persecution, Baptists in both Imperial Russia and the USSR have also benefited from the nation's general socio-economic, educational, and cultural progress. Perhaps this helps to compensate somewhat for the problems associated with the shortage of leaders with formal theological and pastoral training. Overall, the number of leaders with some formal training has increased, despite the fact that such training opportunities are presently less accessible than they were during the first quarter of the twentieth century.

More important than these numerical, social, and educational changes are those features of Russian Baptist life which have remained essentially the same for over one hundred years. The movement emerged and continues to grow in response to popular needs unmet from other quarters. In every walk of life there were those who longed for an understandable, personal, and practical religion, one which offered certainty, compassion, and community, one which demonstrated its spiritual-moral strength in the daily lives of its members. With few exceptions, throughout its history Baptism has continued to draw both its mass membership and its leaders from among the common people. (Of course, it is not exactly true, as Soviet writers argue, that it is chiefly the disadvantaged who become Baptists. Rather, official government policy and practice virtually ensure that those who are Baptists will become disadvantaged.) Baptism's popular-democratic quality is also reflected in its consistent emphasis on church-state separation, the autonomy of the local church, and congregational church government. Persistent congregational solidarity in the face of official and social pressures, mutual aid, and the church as one's life and activity center indicate that this people's movement has maintained a strong corporate emphasis.

This does not mean, however, that the personal aspect is neglected. Members of Baptist churches are such by personal choice, accepted as believer's baptism candidates (immersion) on the basis of combined testimony and a life-style demonstration of personal conversion. Church leaders and fellow-members certainly encourage and challenge the believer to live up to the high calling of the Christian. But, as compared to those, say, in more hierarchical-sacramental churches, Baptists are expected to take more *personal* responsibility for prayer and Bible study, spiritual and moral growth, participation in church government and service, and involvement in evangelism.

This personal/individual emphasis has also been reflected in the impact which highly-gifted leaders have had on sections of the Russian Baptist movement. Thus, the multi-talented Alexander Karev, longtime General Secretary of the Union of Evangelical Christians-Baptists, once paid tribute to his three greatest teachers – Ivan Prokhanov (administration), Ivan Kargel (theology) and William Fetler (evangelism). Karev himself represented a leader's influence in fostering the somewhat broader, "inter-denominational" stream of Russian evangelicalism. This would also include Prokhanov, Kargel, and nineteenth-century evangelical aristocrats such as Colonel Vasily Pashkov and Counts Modest Korff and Alexis Bobrinskii. The more specifically Baptist stance of pre-Revolutionary leaders such as Fetler, Vasily Pavlov, and especially Baptist Union President Dei Mazaev, also has its contemporary representatives. Among those whom we met personally was the former pastor of the large Leningrad church, Sergei Fadukhin.

United on essentials, then as now, strong-minded leaders have differed on less-central matters of faith and practice. These doctrinal-practical differences have been magnified by personality clashes and leadership ambitions. As well, problems have arisen because of the need to work in the context of repressive socio-political conditions during both the Tsarist and Soviet eras. Present-day conflicts, of course, have their unique features. There is no real pre-Revolutionary parallel, for example, to today's state interference in the internal life of the church, with its associated problems. Of these, the most serious are: restraints on Christian education, evangelism, and social service, and the tensions arising from the activities – whether actual or alleged – of "planted" informers and "state-agent" pastors within the Churches. Yet in many ways the contemporary clash between Reformers (President Gennady Kriuchkov, International Representative Georgi Vins) and officials of the original

(1944) Baptist Union (President Andrei Klimenko, General Secretary Alexei Bychkov) is but the latest in a century-long series.

Throughout its history Russian Baptism has been a persecuted church. Feeling threatened by the Baptists' aggressive evangelism, frustrated pre-Revolutionary Orthodox clergy and post-Revolutionary Communist ideologues repeatedly called upon the state to use force against these too-successful rivals. Even apart from these appeals, authoritarian government officials in both eras have considered the Baptists' totalist beliefs to be a threat to social stability, national security, and the régime-approved course of development. Thus, anti-Baptist propagandists over the years have managed to get official and public support (or at least public acceptance) for the use of force against stubborn believers. In order to do so, they have used a variety of rational-scientific and pseudo-scientific arguments. They have also appealed to national loyalties and age-old prejudices, fears, and hatreds.

An impartial consideration of the Baptists' record provides overwhelming proof that the repressive measures were and are unjustifiable. This is true not only on humanitarian grounds, but even on any rational assessment of social stability and national security needs. Of course, in any religious movement there is a gap between the ideals professed and the lives lived by the mass membership. Baptism has also had its share of reprobates, though external pressure and internal church discipline have kept the number of such relatively small. On the other hand, for over one hundred years the overwhelming majority of Baptists have given proof that they are very good citizens, workers, and neighbors. Thus, in actual fact, both state and society would benefit if Baptism were promoted instead of being persecuted.

Though recurrent, persecution has not been uniform, as periods of more intense repression (e.g. 1894–1905, 1929–1939, 1959–1964) have alternated with more relaxed, somewhat freer ones (e.g. 1905–1914, 1917–1929, 1953–1959). Official policy, it seems has been influenced primarily by general domestic and international developments and by the pace and extent of Baptism's growth. Thus, for example, Russia's defeat in the Russo-Japanese War (1904–1905) and the accompanying revolution (1905) forced a shaken tsarist régime to grant an elected assembly and civil liberties. Thanks in part to their improved legal status, Baptists experienced their greatest pre-Revolutionary growth in the decade before 1914. World War I brought intensified Russian nationalism and extreme unity-security consciousness. Those who felt threatened by Baptism's recent growth could take advantage of the wartime atmosphere to charge the allegedly "un-Russian" Baptists with disloyalty.

Similarly, the February Revolution of 1917 which overthrew the tsarist régime re-established and enhanced religious liberty. More concerned with other domestic and international problems and seeing the Baptists as fellow-sufferers under tsarism, the victorious Bolsheviks (October Revolution) also permitted the Baptists considerable freedom. As a result, by 1929 the Baptist community had grown to about four million, with Christian young people's groups claiming a larger membership than the Komsomol (Communist Youth Union). Alarmed at this growth and about to launch the massive "Second Revolution" (collectivization for agriculture, the five-year plans for rapid industrial development), the Stalinist régime began a brutal crackdown on religion generally. The period of Baptism's most extensive growth was followed by the period of its most extreme persecution.

By raising the price of commitment, persecution has contributed to the purity of Russian Baptism. Merely nominal Christians, fearing personal loss, do not want to risk joining a Baptist church. Committed Baptist pastors and church members, concerned about the church's strength and staying power, do not want to risk accepting merely nominal Christians as members of their churches. (Happily, in the USSR there are really no liberal or neo-evangelical Baptist churches to attract the merely nominal or to divide the Baptist movement and to dilute its strength.)

Persecution has made Russian Baptists into second-class citizens, subject to legal and socio-economic discrimination. But this has also meant that they are less subject to the ever-present temptation faced by Western evangelicals – the acceptance and imitation of the outlook, life-style, and methods of the secular society in which they live. Economic and educational deprivation has indeed imposed hardships on Russian Baptists, but this same deprivation has helped them to avoid Western Christianity's chronic diseases of materialism and theological liberalism.

Whatever their differences, Russian Baptists have maintained, for over a century, an evangelical purity of life and belief that is at once inspiration and rebuke. As such, a comparison with Western evangelicalism seems to bear out the truth of the old adage that the church can survive anything except prosperity and popularity.

Ironically, persecution has also helped to make Russian Baptism into a powerful church. Of course, Baptism's power is not of the same nature as, say, that of those former European state churches – the prestige of tradition, wealth, learning, elaborate institutions, socio-economic and political influence. Rather, in both nature and demonstration Baptism's power is essentially spiritual.

It is spiritual power that has enabled Baptism to survive and grow in a hostile environment and also to avoid the ravages of internal decay. The high level of retention of believers' children, the always-crowded services, the dramatically-transformed lives of new converts, congregational solidarity in the face of persecution, the fact that imprisoned believers persistently preach to fellow-prisoners – all give concrete evidence of that power.

And all this is accomplished without the legal statutes, or the financial, educational, publication and media-access resources enjoyed – nay, considered indispensable – by Western evangelicals. Who knows? Perhaps we too would benefit by having more of the disadvantages suffered by Baptists in the USSR!

B. THE RUSSIAN/SOVIET EVANGELICALS: A CHRONO-LOGICAL SURVEY

I. *The Pre-Revolutionary Period*

1813 – establishment of Russian Bible Society; mass circulation of the Scriptures in the commonly-spoken Russian language to 1826 (RBS closed); unofficial distribution by various agencies continues.

1820s to 1860s – recurring revivals in German colonies in South Russia also influence Slavic neighbors.

1860s to mid-1870s – emergence of evangelical movements among Slavic people in Ukraine, Caucasus, St. Petersburg (Influences include: crisis of the old order resulting from defeat in the Crimean War and the death of Nicholas I, together with resultant modernization program and its accompanying opportunities and strains; dissatisfaction with the state Orthodox

Church and other religious groups; increasing literacy and availability of the Scriptures; contacts with German evangelicals and Bible colporteurs in Ukraine and Caucasus; preaching of English evangelist Lord Radstock in St. Petersburg).

1870 – V. G. Pavlov (1854–1924) begins his ministry.

1864/1879/1883 – toleration acts "officially" grant a measure of religious liberty to evangelicals, but discrimination and persecution continue.

1884 – establishment of Russian Baptist Union; (RBU) (includes Germans and Russians; Johann Wieler, first President)

1886 – D. I. Mazaev, President of RBU (with few interruptions, to 1920).

1894 – Stundism (South Russian Baptism) is declared to be "an especially harmful sect"; systematic, intense persecution lasts to about 1903.

1901 – Ivan Prokhanov (1869–1935) begins his multi-faceted ministry in St. Petersburg (while working full time for Westinghouse corporation).

1903 – Tsaritsyn (Stalingrad, now Volgograd) conference unites several evangelical congregations into "The Union of Evangelical Christians-Baptists".

1905 – First Russian Revolution forces Nicholas II to grant a constitution, elected assembly, civil liberties; period of rapid growth of evangelicals in numbers, publication, organizational strength; Russian Baptist delegation attends first congress of Baptist World Alliance (1905), London.

1907 – William Fetler (1883–1957) begins his dynamic ministry in St. Petersburg.

1909 – Prokhanov organizes Union of Evangelical Christians as an alternative to older Baptist Union; government circulars curb religious liberties granted in 1905–6; increasing repression.

1911 – Prokhanov elected as one of ten vice-presidents of the Baptist World Alliance at Philadelphia congress; Fetler opens the 2000-seat Baptist church, *Dom Evangelia* (House of the Gospel) in St. Petersburg.

1914–1917 – Russia in World War I; Baptist-Evangelical Christian community of approximately 500,000 experiences discrimination and persecution, labelled as "un-Russian" and disloyal by their religious-political opponents; conversions of hundreds of Russian soldiers in German p. o. w. camps.

1917 – February Revolution overthrows tsarist regime and re-establishes, enhances religious liberty; victorious Bolsheviks (October Revolution) initially maintain this policy towards evangelicals.

II. *The Soviet Period*

A. *The Lenin era (1917–1924)*

– establishment of the Bolshevik dictatorship, separate peace with Germany, attempt to establish a purely socialist economic system lead to Allied military intervention and four years of devastating civil war; (Bolshevik victory; modifying of the economic system to permit some private and co-operative enterprise).

1918 – decrees separating church and state, church and school; constitution guarantees freedom of religion and of both religious and anti-religious propaganda (also in 1924 constitution).

– committed to the eventual elimination of all religion, Bolsheviks' methods include: the use of force, legislation, and "educational" activity through schools, special atheist organizations, child and youth groups, the mass media.

– *rapid growth of the evangelical movement continues to 1928/9.* (appeal of the message and life-style in an atmosphere of turbulent change, legal privileges, return of leaders from exile and imprisonment, organizational development, activity of returned "soldier-evangelists"); failure of recurrent attempts to unite Baptists and Evangelical Christians into a single union.

B. *The Stalin Era (1924–1953)*

1928/9 Stalin launches the "Second Revolution" (collectivization in agriculture, five-year plans for rapid industrialization); extreme pressures on all sectors of Soviet society; end to the relative freedom and diversity of the 1920s as Stalin endeavors to establish a monolithic communist-atheist society).

1928 – Prokhanov leaves USSR.

1929 – law on religious associations establishes detailed regulations for registration, conduct of religious activity, relationship of churches to government bodies; severe restrictions on extra-church activities, evangelism, Christian education, social services; dropping of former privilege of religious propaganda (only *anti-religious* propaganda permitted – same principle included in 1936 and 1977 Constitutions).

1934–1939 – period of the Great Terror, a nightmare of mass arrests, imprisonment, executions involving millions; (of 25,000 Baptists arrested

in the period 1929–1945, on
the prison camp experience).

1935 – Baptist Union central activity (
Evangelical Christians continu
services.

1941–1945 – USSR in World War II . . . terrible
devastation, loss of twenty million lives; virtual disappearance of open activity by evangelicals until 1943.

1944 – state pressure accomplishes what Baptists and
Evangelical Christians had thus far failed to do
as the two groups are united under the name
"The Union of Evangelical Christ-
ians-Baptists" (Iakov Zhidkov, President;
Alexander Karev, General Secretary); some
Pentecostal churches (after 1945) join the
Union, along with a number of Mennonite
congregations and some few other evangelical
churches.

1945 – Union begins publication of *Bratskii Vestnik*
(*Brotherly Messenger*); outbreak of spontaneous
revivals, mass conversions in a number of
places.

1948 – as part of Stalin's Iron Curtain response to the
Cold War, Russian Baptists' contacts with
foreign co-religionists are stopped; government crackdown on unregistered congregations.

1949 – *Bratskii Vestnik* ceases publication.

1953 – death of Stalin and beginning of the "thaw";
return of some prisoners; resumption of publication of *Bratskii Vestnik*.

C. *The Krushchev Era* (1953–1964)

1954 – Russian Baptist leaders begin to travel in the
West.

1956 – Khrushchev's de-Stalinization speech; return of huge numbers of prisoners; beginning of another period of spontaneous revival and mass conversions.

1959–1964 – Khrushchev's anti-religious campaign of stepped-up propaganda, arrests and imprisonment, closing of one-half of the Baptist (and Orthodox) churches.

1960 – All-Union Council of Evangelical Christians-Baptists issues "Letter of Instructions" and proposed constitutional changes (calling for curbs on aggressive evangelism, Christian education, young people's work, charitable activity; advocating more centralized administrative system); strong protests and demands for the calling of a reform congress by the *Initsiativniki* ("Men of Initiative").

1962 – Organizational Committee of Reformers plans for an All-Union Congress of the Evangelical Christian-Baptist Churches; Committee excommunicates 27 of the top ECB leaders.

1963 – AUCECB congress agrees to some modification of the 1960 letter and constitutional proposals.

D. *The Brezhnev Era (1964–1982)*

1964 – ouster of Khrushchev; temporary relaxation of anti-religious pressures; Reformers set up Council of Prisoners' Relatives to petition and publicize; (about 200 Baptists in prison on the average during any given year, from 1960s to mid-1970s).

1965 – beginning of crackdown on dissidents generally by Brezhnev-Kosygin regime; Reformers' Organizational Committee is re-constituted as

"The Union of Churches of Evangelical Christians- Baptists", an alternative to the older (1944) Union.

1966 – Reform leader Georgi Vins sentenced to three years' imprisonment.

1968 – Council of Prisoners' Relatives reports that unregistered churches are caring for 2000 dependents of 300 persecuted believers.

1969 – Tula conference of new Council of Churches of ECB; no reconciliation between Reformers and old Union. Union Congress seen as a turning point toward congregational polity.

1971 – Reformers announce establishment of printing agency *Khristianin* ("The Christian"); first issue of *Bulletin of Council of Prisoners' Relatives*.

1972 – beginning of Soviet-US détente is accompanied by *increased* pressures on dissidents; (from 1963–1976, one unregistered congregation in Leningrad had all of its meetings broken up by the police; murder of Baptist soldier Ivan Moiseyev, 1972).

1974 – Union Baptist congress sees a group of 50 from Union churches calling for election of worthy leaders, and removal of undeserving; arrest of Georgi Vins.

1975 – Helsinki Agreement raises hopes for freer East-West contacts and greater civil liberties in USSR, but Soviets use Helsinki "escape clause" i.e.: "agreement is subordinate to each nation's own constitution and law code"; new regulations impose further limits on even private, family religious instruction of children; tightening of registration and building regulations administration; state pressing

Reform congregations to register; Georgi Vins sentenced to 5 years in prison camp plus 5 years' exile; publication of a petition (1,147 signatures) protesting against harassment of believers' children and removal from their homes to be enrolled in state boarding schools.

1976 – reports of some easing of anti-religious pressures; gradual decrease of numbers of those in prison to an average of 40–50 by later 1970s; Reformers issue list of 14 Baptists who died under mysterious circumstances, 1962–1976.

1979 – Reform leader Georgi Vins and family permitted to leave USSR in exchange for US-held Soviet agents, Soviet invasion of Afghanistan.

1980 – US-led boycott of 1980 Moscow Olympics and election of Reagan heighten East-West tensions; increasing pressures against evangelicals.

1982 – death of Brezhnev; replaced by Iurii Andropov (former KGB chief); increased repression continues, with the number of Baptists imprisoned by the mid-1980s rising to approximately 200.

1: *On Stepping into the Same River Twice*

As the Air France plane began its descent on the Leningrad airport, memories of my 1971 visit to the USSR tumbled through my mind. On that occasion I had been doing historical research at the university library in Helsinki, Finland. Leningrad was so near geographically that it seemed foolish not to spend a week-end there – whatever the additional strain on a graduate student's already strained finances. But Leningrad might be very far off bureaucratically, since Soviet officialdom could be maddeningly slow.

After some to-the-dollar calculations I had worked out a plan. By taking the Thursday evening train from Helsinki and the late Sunday night train back I could have three full days in Leningrad, while having to pay for only two nights. Breakfasts were included in the package and I could substitute cheap snack foods for restaurant meals. Half-doubtfully, I had presented my suggestions to a Finnish travel agent. Both of us were amazed when Intourist (official Soviet travel bureau) answered affirmatively – and within one week.

I was ready hours before the eight o'clock departure time, anxious to board the dark-green railway carriage with its Russian-language identification which I had quickly found on arrival at the station. I was also anxious about the customs check at the Soviet border. Under the clothing, toiletries, camera, extra film, and Leningrad guide-book in my bulging briefcase, there were three

Russian-language New Testaments.

"Are you also going to Leningrad?" The question had come, in slightly-accented English, from a swarthy, well-dressed man about forty years of age. In response to my affirmative reply he had gone on to introduce himself as an engineer from Yugoslavia, returning home via the USSR from a recent conference in Helsinki. Would I mind if he travelled with me as far as Leningrad?

We shared tea and conversation during the early part of that all-night train ride. After an hour or so I asked him off-handedly why he had spoken to me in English on coming up to me at the railway station, since we had almost immediately switched to Russian. The easy conversational flow gave way to a strained silence. Obviously embarrassed, he sputtered out some vague, disjointed fragments, chiefly intended to prevent further questioning. But we soon returned to less embarrassing topics such as family, education and religion. Though brought up in a religious home, he had become a convinced atheist through scientific study. Mathematics, he insisted, explained all natural phenomena – including, apparently, his love for the attractive wife and children in the picture which he had shown me. The entire universe, he declared triumphantly was one perfectly orderly, mathematically exact system. Innocently, I asked him what made this perfectly orderly universe so orderly. "But . . . but . . . that's *religion!*" he snorted derisively, presumably unable to answer my simple question.

At about three a.m. our train had reached the Finnish-Soviet border. Brandishing automatic rifles, the guards began to examine the train's undercarriage. Were they searching for smuggled goods or for people trying to enter the USSR illegally? Surely it would be more logical to look for hidden people on trains *leaving* the USSR.

Customs officers then worked their way through the

compartments. Perfectly relaxed, my Yugoslav acquaintance commented sympathetically on my own evident nervousness. He chatted comfortably, like an old friend, with the surprisingly pleasant customs officer, after which the now less pleasant-looking officer turned to me.

My travel documents proved to be in order and the amount of foreign currency I was carrying in a makeshift money belt was duly recorded. I was beginning to breathe more easily when the officer asked abruptly if I had any literature. As casually as I could, I showed him the English-language guidebook to Leningrad. Unfortunately, he would not be put off so easily and insisted on searching my briefcase. With eyes gleaming triumphantly, he quickly pulled out my three Russian-language New Testaments. "We do not permit this kind of literature to enter our country," he barked.

My protests that the New Testaments were for personal use were ignored. He scribbled a few words on an official-looking form and handed it over for me to sign. Unable to make out much beyond the notation "three Russian-language New Testaments" and anxious about the unknown consequences of my attempt at Bible smuggling, I hesitated.

"Sign it," he said, in a somewhat less intimidating tone. "It's merely to verify that we confiscated this illegal literature."

Half-agreeing, half-doubtful, I began to scrawl a signature, my hand moving jerkily in response to contradictory signals from my brain. The officer watched, with the straight line of his thin lips bent upwards – a bare millimetre or so – at each end. I handed over the single sheet of coarse paper, not even thinking to ask for a copy of this police document. He tucked the incriminating form safely into an inside pocket and stalked out.

At long last the train began to move and I began to calm down. The calmness shaded into confidence as I remembered certain encouraging rumors. It seems that enterprising customs officers sometimes sell confiscated Bibles on the black market at 100 rubles ($160 Canadian) a copy. Deliciously ironic too was the overall picture of a super-power, capable of destroying the world, yet feeling threatened by three little books.

After the border crossing my formerly-talkative travelling companion had very little to say. We sat in silence as the train moved swiftly through pine forests and occasional villages. And this mysterious Yugoslav engineer, apparently bound for Leningrad, disappeared before we reached that city.

There were hundreds of people crowding the platforms at Leningrad's Finland station. I stood there for several minutes, expecting to be met by some paper-clutching clerk, who would tell me what to do next. None came. Where was the celebrated "We-know-your-every-move" system? Approaching a uniformed man, I identified myself as a Canadian tourist and asked where I should go.

"To the Hotel Astoria," he replied. "That's where they all go."

"And how do I get there?" I asked, not yet having mastered the guidebook map.

"Taxi!" he grunted, presumably wondering if all Canadian tourists were as dumb as this one seemed to be.

I walked out into the square, dominated by a statue of Lenin which commemorated the historic arrival of the founder of the USSR at this same railway station in April, 1917. It was a short ride across the Neva river, past the magnificent Winter Palace and the Admiralty, whose spire, along with the dome of St. Isaac's Cathedral, still dominates the Leningrad skyline. Circling the imposing equestrian statue of Tsar Nicholas I (1825–1855), we jolted to a stop in front of the Astoria.

"One ruble, fifty," the driver announced as I swung out of the taxi.

Anxious to get going from the railway station, I had neglected to exchange Western for Soviet currency. Would he take some Finnish marks? No, that was not permitted. A few seconds of looking helplessly at one another, an exchange of "What now?" and mutual shoulder shrugging produced no solution. Mouthing some harsh Russian curses, he left in an angry cloud of black exhaust smoke.

A bit shaken, I walked up to the reception counter and presented my passport and travel documents. "Nesdoly," the clerk repeated slowly to herself as she checked the reservation list. "No, we don't have you registered here. Could you wait a moment, please?"

Several phone calls later she still had no idea where I was registered. Finally, after an animated conversation with some Intourist official, she smiled triumphantly. "All settled. You are to go to the Hotel Leningrad. Sit right there, don't go anywhere. *We* will get you a taxi." Despite the frustrations and the wasting of potential sightseeing time I was beginning to enjoy the experience. So this was yet another example of the all-knowing Soviet system in action.

The young taxi driver spoke freely. Had I experienced any difficulty in getting into the Soviet Union? How did that difficulty compare with the problems involved in crossing the Canadian-US border. He shook his head sadly as I endeavored to compare walls and doorways. "Unfortunately, they don't let us travel at all freely," he sighed. "Tell me frankly," he continued, "do Canadians live well?" I assured him that despite ups-and-downs in the economy, Canadian workers live fairly well, with various forms of social welfare measures to carry them through the problems of unemployment, sickness, and old age. "We would have better living standards here too," he responded, "if we had not suffered so much during the war. And the USSR sends so much of its wealth to the East European states, you know. Why, we practically support them!"

I had no time to point out that other countries had also suffered from the destruction of 1939–45, a generation ago, or that some scholars would argue that East European states gave more than they received. We had arrived at the Hotel Leningrad, a huge modern-looking structure. Ironically, it was only a few blocks from the Finland Station, where I had arrived almost two hours earlier.

Confidently, I approached the desk, announcing that I was Nesdoly, the Canadian tourist. The clerk was polite, but uncomprehending, as she scanned the reservation list. I was not registered. Endeavoring to be helpful, I informed her that I had been specifically sent over here from the Astoria. A buzz of conversation followed with a couple of equally-uncomprehending fellow-clerks and then the poor girl was back to where I waited at the counter.

"I wonder why they sent you here," she asked rather pathetically.

We stood there, doing a kind of re-run of my earlier scene with the unpaid taxi driver. And then I heard those wonderful words which no one in the Soviet bureaucracy ever used, "I will take full responsibility. Give him a room!"

Smiling in the midst of my day-dreaming recollections, I remembered the contrast between that hotel's exterior and interior. Built only one and one-half years prior to my 1971 visit, it had the rundown appearance of so many Soviet buildings – peeling wallpaper, spotted and worn-through carpets, stained ceilings. But most of all I remembered my first attempt at having a bath. Considerable pressure had to be exerted before the taps would turn. Nothing happened for a few seconds. Then came a rumbling gurgle followed by an explosive gush of a blackish liquid. After a half-minute of this the water eventually cleared to about the colour of weak tea and seemed unlikely to improve. But after an exhausting day of sight-seeing I was grateful for the opportunity to soak – or to steep, as the case might be.

The bump as we landed jolted me out of the memories of June, 1971 and into the present reality of May, 1978. The Canadian graduate, student, tourist had returned as a visiting scholar under the Canada-USSR Academic Exchange Program. From her window seat, my wife, Lil, had been viewing the northern landscape through her artist's eyes. I was eager to begin showing her the beauties of Leningrad, the "Venice of the North", with its splendid museums and art galleries. Having her with me to share impressions and experiences would be a wonderful complement to my research work in libraries and archives.

The plane stopped and we quickly gathered our carry-on luggage, anxious to salvage the remainder of this warm Saturday afternoon. It proved to be a very warm Saturday afternoon, what with the air conditioning turned off and a thirty-minute delay in de-planing.

We were greeted by a half-dozen officials, annoyed at the three-hour lateness of the Air France arrival and more than ready to go home. Grim faces and curt, snappish questions gave the exuberant French tourists their first sobering taste of life in the USSR. For those with children, however, the officials had nothing but engaging smiles, sympathetic cooings, and the winning charm we had always associated with all our older Slavic relatives.

"Delighted to see this display of the traditional Russian heart," we said to the motherly-looking woman who directed us to the customs official.

"Of course, of course," she replied, smiling warmly. "How can anyone not respond to the needs of children, especially when they're so tired after a long trip from Paris?"

"So you are of Russian descent, from Canada? Welcome to our country. This way, please."

Face to face, our customs official also seemed to be less abrupt, more human than the ones we had observed earlier back in the line. Almost casually he asked a few simple questions. Our luggage, including the bag containing fifteen Russian New Testaments, went by unopened.

"Are you the Canadian professor?" asked a rather nondescript man, who came up to us after virtually all the other passengers had left.

"Yes," I answered, a little disappointed. "Are you with the University of Leningrad?"

"Well," he chuckled, "the university sent me, but I am just a taxi driver. Those your bags? I'll drive you to your hotel – the Oktiabrskaia."

"At least they know that we're here," I muttered to Lil as we drove past row after weary row of monotonously identical apartment blocks. Up ahead was a police van, with a couple of officers vigorously assisting a barely-mobile Soviet proletarian across the street.

"Another guy that'll be 25 rubles poorer by tomorrow," our driver informed us cheerfully. "That's the usual fine – about three days' wages – for being drunk and disorderly. But, you should realize," he went on, "that many of the drunks you will see are not our people. They are Finns from Helsinki, who come to Leningrad for the cheap vodka!"

[8]

That provocative statement would have to go unchallenged – about the proportion of Finns and Russians, for example – since we had arrived at the hotel, located on Leningrad's main street, Nevsky Prospekt. "Professor and Mrs. Nesdoly, from Canada," I announced half-heartedly to the attractive woman, about thirty years old, behind the reception desk.

"Welcome to Leningrad," she responded brightly. "We expected you earlier in the afternoon. Your plane was three hours late? That's a shame – you must be very tired."

Somewhat overcome by the contrast with my previous visit, I asked if the room was ready and where I could obtain some Soviet currency. She looked puzzled by the first question. Of course the room was ready and had been for hours. Her reply to my second request was even more heartening. Unfortunately the currency exchange was closed until tomorrow morning, but she would personally lend me five roubles so that we could get something to eat. Clearly, coming on the academic exchange program did make a difference.

A quick meal of bread, cold chicken, cucumbers and tea in the hotel's buffet room was followed by an hour of enjoyable, commercial-free television in a comfortable hotel room. Our weary bodies were grateful for the large, old-fashioned bathtub and the immediate abundance of hot and sparkling clean water. Our wet bodies became somewhat marginally less so after half-hearted dabbing with the dishtowel-like things which we found on the towel rack.

2: *A Return Visit to Poklonaia Gora*

We had slept well, despite the unusual near-midnight sunshine and a rather exuberant wedding celebration directly below us in the hotel's reception room. Now, on a familiar-looking bus, we were rattling along toward the registered Union Baptist church on Poklonaia Gora in the northern part of this city of four million. "Much easier than in 1971," I said to Lil.

Prior to my first visit to Leningrad, a Russian pastor in Helsinki had told me the location of the church, but not how to get there from my hotel. Surely, I thought, an important landmark such as Poklonaia Gora, commemorating Charles XII of Sweden's defeat by the victorious Peter the Great of Russia in 1709, would be known by every Leningrader. Now, with so many tourists wanting to visit the city's one registered Baptist church, any hotel clerk would be able to give me directions.

Unfortunately, the clerk at the Hotel Leningrad, presumably not wanting to collaborate in any kind of religious activity, had not been very helpful. "Poklonaia Gora? Oh, you'll have to take a bus, then catch the train, and at last either take a taxi or walk. It is very far!" she concluded, obviously hoping that I would not insist on pursuing the matter. Puzzled, I had gone sightseeing, determined to ask someone else.

The next morning, I had casually asked directions from a few Russians lounging in the hotel lobby. "Poklonaia Gora? Very straightforward," said one of them, pointing out the window. "Catch a number 75 bus in front of the Finland Station over there and simply get off at the end of the run, which is Poklonaia Gora."

The bus was crowded, making it necessary for me to stand next to an obviously intoxicated Soviet worker. He must have started out early, considering that it was still only nine a.m. Presumably my Western-style clothes identified me unmistakably as a tourist. As a patriotic Soviet citizen, he considered it his duty to be helpful, and thus he informed me politely, if somewhat boozily, that I was on the wrong bus. My reply, assuring him that I was on the right bus, was brushed aside somewhat less politely.

"Nothing to see where this bus goes," he burbled. "Better switch to the bus that goes to the Piskarevskoe Cemetery, honoring those who died in the siege of Leningrad."

"No thanks," I replied, trying to end an unpleasant conversation. "I think I'll stay on this bus for now."

"Aha, so you're going to the church!", he wheezed, moving even closer and, unfortunately, breathing heavily and damply into my face. "Never mind," he half-snarled, "we're going to blow the place up and build a factory there."

"But," I protested, "what of the oft-repeated Soviet boast that freedom of religious worship is constitutionally guaranteed?"

He snorted contemptuously, collapsing into a recently-vacated seat. Then, as if explaining a simple truth to a not very bright student, he concluded: "In the USSR we have separation of church and state, thus giving us the power to do anything we want!"

Admittedly, official policy would be stated with somewhat more attention to coherence and logic. But the end result, unfortunately, was often not very different – forced closure, rather than simple destruction of church buildings.

The bus stopped and so did my daydreaming reminiscences. Along with about a dozen others, Lil and I began our walk along a dusty road leading toward the familiar green-domed building. Formerly an Orthodox church, it was now the meeting place of the 3,000-member Baptist congregation.

My first impression was that much remained the same as it had been on my previous visit. There was still enough seating space for only about half of the 10 a.m. congregation of approximately 900. Once again, foreign visitors were ushered into front seats or on to the platform. Women seemed to outnumber men by about two to one, with older people predominating.

Here and there, bright-eyed and brightly-dressed children, together with their teenaged and early-twenties brothers and sisters, indicated that some changes had occurred. Commenting on this, one of the 30 preaching brethren informed us that there had been only about 40 young people in the congregation in 1971, but this had increased to some 400 by 1978.

Bibles and hymnbooks were still in short supply, though conditions had improved considerably over the seven years. Gifts from abroad had supplemented the very inadequate officially-permitted publications. *Na levo* (literally, "on the left") there were black-market purchases and the products of the Baptists' own very "unofficial" publishing network.

Dynamic little Sergei Fadukhin, the senior pastor, was still preaching powerful sermons, characterized by a superb use of illustrations and very pointed application of Biblical principles to contemporary Soviet life conditions. Two other brethren would also bring short messages, seeking, by their simplicity, urgency, and repetition, to drive one solid shaft of truth deep down into the hearts of their earnest listeners.

On that occasion, and for the next two weeks, the Easter message would be central. Along with other East European Christians, the Russian Baptists place an especially strong emphasis on Easter generally and Christ's resurrection in particular. Though not at all neglecting the cross and atonement for sin, they stress the importance of resurrection power to live a victorious Christian life. Along with the purifying effects of persecution and the moral strength of a tightly-bound Christian community, this resurrection power emphasis helps to explain the tremendous spiritual vitality of the Baptists in the USSR.

Typical of this resurrection emphasis was a simple chorus which we heard at least a dozen times. Sung slowly to a traditional minor melody, yet joyously, by those who knew the reality of resurrection power, the impact was overwhelming.

> *Christ has risen from the dead!*
> *Through death, He conquered death!*
> *To those who dwelt among the graves*
> *Eternal life he gave!*

Between messages, the slow congregational singing of familiar hymns took us back to half-forgotten childhood scenes of Russian Baptist services in rural Saskatchewan. We had choirs then as well, but nothing to compare with those we heard here. After all, the best of their four choirs bore the name traditionally associated with excellence: the Academy Choir.

They had sung a special after-church concert for me in 1971, consisting of six numbers from the 100th-anniversary cantata. I had been thrilled by the superb quality of their singing on that special occasion. Now we would discover that their regular musical minis-

[13]

try – consisting of four or five anthems during a typical two-hour service – was equally impressive.

Among other things, their working repertoire must have been extensive indeed. As the preacher delivered his message, the choir director leafed through a pile of books, looking for the number which would best complement the speaker's theme. We watched in fascination. A whispered title and a series of nods of recognition is followed by a barely-perceptible turning of pages. The pastor announces simply that the choir will sing. The pianist strikes a chord. Eyes riveted on the conductor, 60 powerful voices soar to the heavenlies in a complex harmony of exquisitely-directed praise.

I had tried to describe to Lil the experience of hearing a Russian Baptist congregation at prayer, but in the words of the old adage, some things are 'better felt than tell't'. Though several were eager to lead out, the initial outburst of four or five *O Gospodi's* ("Oh Lord!") quickly changed to a single voice, leading a chorus of reverent, sibilant, whispered outpourings of individual, yet also collective heart-cries. It was like the sea symphony, heard on the shores of the Bay of Fundy, back home in far-off Nova Scotia – both majestic and intimate, at once ceaseless movement and tranquillity, bewildering diversity and yet one awe-inspiring whole. And when the one leading in prayer called on God in mercy to forgive sin and to bring salvation to their children, an ocean of terrible anguish and triumphant faith swelled into a great crashing wave of *Da Gospodi!* ("Yes, Lord!").

There were visitors today, a delegation of Baptists and Pentecostals from Hungary. Skilled interpreters translated the messages and reports from Magyar (and, surprisingly, English) into Russian. The congregation listened intently. Beaming faces and periodic exclamations of *Slava Bogu* (Glory to God) testified to their appreciation of the Christian solidarity expressed by this visit. At the close of the service, Lil and I, as honored guests, were invited to share lunch with the Hungarian visitors in the church basement.

We soon found our heads swivelling as we tried to respond to the many eager questioners. What church did we attend? Did we know Brother — ? Had we ever met the Poysti brothers? (No!) Did we perhaps know David Borisovich Weins? (Yes!) "You know him personally – and he was even instrumental in Lil's conversion? *Slava Bogu!* Do pass on to him our deep appreciation for his shortwave radio broadcasts. The reverent music is especially uplifting. But perhaps you could tell him to check on the broadcasting facilities. Most of the program comes through very clearly, but for some reason we generally get a sudden increase in static levels when he begins the message."

Another insistent voice. "Do you live anywhere near the town of — ? Perhaps, then, you know my sister," he continued, in response to our reply, indicating that we knew his nephew very well. "Could you, perhaps, take a picture of my family to send to my sister on your return to Canada?"

He was one of the thirty preaching brethren in the Leningrad church and could thus provide much additional information about current conditions. I knew, for example, that Soviet regulations prohibit public religious instruction of children. Yet here were his own three little girls, along with many other children at the church service. Had there been any change in the regulations?

"Not officially," he answered, "but for some time the enforcement of that regulation has been lax."

He nodded in agreement at my suggestion that the Reform Baptists' refusal to bow to Soviet pressure tactics in this area had been a factor. "So," I continued, "are you now able to hold regular children's Sunday School classes?" He was silent for a moment, looking around carefully at the circle of those watching our picture-taking.

"No," he said quietly, "things are not yet as free as that, but we find various ways to supplement the Christian instruction which we all give in our homes."

Intrigued, I was about to ask for some specifics, but a number of additional people had moved within earshot. The change in his expression was subtle, but the message of that change was loud and clear. Further conversation on this interesting subject would have to be postponed.

The lunch was hearty – chunks of dark rye bread and a meaty borshch, cutlets with potatoes and vegetables, fresh fruit, a special Leningrad torte, and tea. The bustling sisters beamed with pleasure as we complimented them on their cooking. Despite what we considered to be heroic efforts on our part, they shook their heads sadly, insisting that we had not really eaten enough. The conversation was equally rich. Our long-unused Russian language skills were put to the test and proved to be less than satisfactory. Fortunately, we could make use of Adam, a translator of English-language scientific articles, who had been seated at the same table.

"The Toronto *Globe and Mail*," he observed, "which I have seen on occasion in our hotels – a bourgeois paper, is it not?"

Groping for words, I tried to explain. How could one use the single label *bourgeois* to cover the range of opinions expressed by staff writers in that paper, to say nothing of the letters to the editor? The endeavor to place my comments within the context of Western concepts of freedom of the press seemed to make matters even more confusing. All of my table mates listened attentively, but their uniformly blank expressions showed that none had understood.

"I have also seen that paper," another church official interjected. Then, holding thumb and forefinger about an inch apart, he added in amazement, "It's that thick!" An incredulous church member, brought up on *Pravda*'s four-to-six-page coverage of all the news that's fit to print, was dumbfounded. What could they be possibly putting into that bourgeois paper? The thickness-measurer, with the confident air of one who knows, looked sympathetically at his naive brother and gave the definitive reply: "Oh, a lot of old women's gossip, as we say!"

The Hungarian visitors had spoken enthusiastically about the blessings and successes of the recent Billy Graham meetings in Budapest. At lunch, one of the older Hungarian Baptist leaders privately expressed his reservations to us. Christian groups, which had been meeting secretly, had been urged to attend the Graham meetings and to be recognized and represented publicly. Accepting as genuine the official promises of greater religious liberty in the future, some of these groups had agreed. The unfortunate result had been a severe government crackdown on the no-longer-secret meetings of these same groups. "And," our table-mate concluded softly, "I'm not surprised when you say that the Western world did not hear of this particular result of the Graham meetings."

As the evening service drew to a close, Pastor Fadukhin announced that it was time to bid the Hungarian guests farewell in the unique Leningrad Baptist manner. The poignant strains of "God Be With You Till We Meet Again" stirred memory-echoes of childhood days, but we were not prepared for what happened as we began the final verse. Nearly a thousand white handkerchiefs suddenly appeared, fluttering like a flock of gentle doves of peace.

Twelve hours after leaving our hotel, we started back toward the bus stop, tired but reluctant to leave this spiritual feasting-place. But the feasting was not yet over.

An enthusiastic church official stopped us at the door, insisting that we join the Hungarian visitors for a light snack. The term 'light snack' proved to be most inappropriate. Once again we ate heroically, and once again the stalwart Russian sisters spoke with true Christian compassion about these feeble efforts by weaker Western brethren.

Small gifts were passed out to the Hungarian visitors, and I was given a huge Leningrad souvenir ballpoint pen. "To assist you in your task of writing the history of our brotherhood," a smiling chairman of the executive council announced. "And now, brother," he continued, "perhaps you could give us a few words."

Haltingly, I thanked them for their many expressions of Christian hospitality, not only that day, but also during my brief visit in 1971. On that occasion, I had heard Russian Baptist history sung by the choir and had met a brother from Tbilisi (Tiflis) in Georgia, one of the cradles of the Russian Baptist movement. It was there that Nikita Voronin, considered to be the first Russian Baptist, had been baptized in 1867. A century later, grandchildren and great-grandchildren were still members of the Tbilisi church, along with 2,000 other believers. Similarly, my grandfather had begun his ministry in the 1890s in Kiev province, continuing for over 60 years in North America. Now, in addition to being a university professor, his grandson was a Baptist pastor. Truly God had begun a good work and would certainly complete it.

"And now," I concluded, "comparing my 1971 visit with this one, I am reminded of the wedding at Cana of Galilee. Then, I was with you for one day, but now I shall be in Leningrad for three weeks. Then I was alone, but now I have brought my dear wife with me. Is this not a clear example of saving the best wine for the last?" Appreciative chuckles indicated that, unlike my attempt at classifying the *Globe and Mail*, these remarks had been understood.

Discussion on the subject of the Graham meetings was revived, stimulated and intensified by rumors that Graham would be coming to the USSR to preach at some time in the future. Turning to a couple of the most enthusiastic of the Hungarian reporters, Pastor Fadukhin stated quietly that he would like to ask a few questions. First, who paid the considerable expenses of the entire Graham visit?

"One can answer that directly and simply," one of the visitors replied. "All was paid for by the Graham organization."

"Good, very good," Fadukhin responded. "My second question is to all of you brethren. You speak of God's blessings on these meetings and of many conversions. As evangelical pastors, Baptists and Pentocostals, could you please tell me how many of these converts have since become baptized members of your churches?" The smiles faded rather abruptly and an embarrassing silence followed. Finally, another one of the visitors raised his head. His eyes met Fadukhin's steady, but not unkind gaze.

"One can also answer that question directly and simply. There have been none." The others nodded in agreement.

"Well, then," Fadukhin said softly, "I have no further questions."

3: *Business as Usual*

"This is your stop," I announced to Lil as the bus continued along Nevsky Prospekt. I had some details of business to attend to at the University of Leningrad and Lil was planning to spend part of the day at the Hermitage.

Formerly the tsars' Winter Palace, this magnificent building on the left bank of the Neva River was now one of the world's great museums and art galleries. We would meet back at the hotel later in the afternoon to share experiences, including Lil's reaction to the score of Rembrandts in a single room, or to the breathtaking gold and white salon, with its dazzling array of huge crystal chandeliers. Clearly, we would have to make several visits to the Hermitage. Some enterprising Soviet statistician had calculated that half-minute stops before each display would add up to a total of nine years before everything could be viewed.

I got off the bus in front of the old Stock Exchange building on Vasilevsky Island, pausing to examine the massive columns with their ship-hull decoration, and to admire the majestic green and white façade of the Hermitage. It was only a short walk from here to the University – most enjoyable too with the mid-morning sunshine sparkling on the Neva's waters and illuminating the multi-hued buildings, constructed when Leningrad was St. Petersburg.

The young man in the International Department

quickly located my file and we reviewed the specifics of my project. Did I know when I would be going to Moscow and Kiev? His office would arrange transportation, of course, but, as specified in the exchange program, I would have to pay for Lil's travel. My travel costs would be paid, along with the provision of hotel accommodation in the three cities. Regrettably, the maximum daily hotel rate under the exchange program was twenty rubles. In Leningrad, therefore, I would have to pay an additional few rubles per day, but there would be no extra charges at Moscow's University hotel. I would receive twelve rubles per day for living expenses, with the first installment available immediately and the second just before we left Leningrad. Passes for the various libraries would also be provided, but the director would have to sign them and he would not be in for a while. In the meantime, I could collect this month's stipend.

By the time I returned from the cashier's office, the library passes had been signed. Pleasantly surprised at this relatively quick settling of what I expected would take much longer, I decided to walk to the Saltykov-Shchedrin Library.

There seemed to be considerably more traffic than I remembered from my previous visit, though nothing comparable to that in a Western city with a fraction of Leningrad's four million people. Perhaps the surprisingly light traffic made me too careless. After a few near misses, I began to wonder if some Leningrad drivers looked on pedestrians as annoying obstacles or tempting targets.

The shops on Nevsky Prospekt were much better stocked than they had been in 1971 and the crowds of people more attractively dressed. Young women in brightly-colored frocks stood out in sharp contrast against the plodding background of older people in heavy, dark clothing. Here and there bobbing flashes of interesting hair colors – ranging from near-orange to near-purple – proved conclusively that it was not only their hairdressers who "knew for sure".

Street vendors were selling *pirozhki* (meat-filled fried pastries) at 15 kopecks (about 20 cents) apiece. A couple of them provided a filling main course, and a wonderfully rich ice cream sandwich at the same price, dessert. I smiled to myself, remembering Churchill's amazement on seeing the Muscovites happily eating ice cream on the streets during a bitterly cold day. He decided that so hardy a people could never be conquered by Hitler or anyone else.

I turned off Nevsky into a square dominated by the statue commemorating the accomplishments of Empress Catherine the Great (1762–96), during whose reign Russia acquired her western and southern provinces. Promoter of education and Russian literature, she would have been pleased with the scene that day. The square was filled with hundreds of people eagerly buying books on every imaginable subject from dozens of overflowing tables which formed a square within the square. Knowing how cheaply books could be bought, I was sorely tempted, but the crowds at each table made it difficult to get close enough to check the titles. Half-reluctantly, I entered the library, an impressive building running virtually the length of the square itself.

In a few minutes I was out on the street again. The clerk had been polite, but insistent, and her superior had been equally unyielding. I could not be admitted to the Library. Certainly, I had the appropriate pass, duly signed and bearing an official stamp. Admittedly, this could be considered as proof that I was indeed a visiting Canadian scholar, part of the Canada-USSR Academic Exchange Program. But the regulations required that I must present my passport. I had left that at the hotel desk?

That was unfortunate, but rules were rules and she could do nothing about it.

I strolled along Nevsky toward the hotel, having decided that it would not be worthwhile to get my passport and return for the hour or so before closing time. Lil would probably be back by now, I thought to myself as I paused in front of the former Cathedral of Our Lady of Kazan, modelled after St. Peter's in Rome. It is now the Museum of the History of Religion and Atheism. In addition to its propagandistic displays, it includes a library, containing rare sources pertaining to my research into Russian Baptist history. But both the displays and the library would have to wait for another day.

Lil had had a few frustrations as well, since the Hermitage was closed on Mondays. But she had enjoyed her visit to Senate Square, with its equestrian statue of the founder of St. Petersburg, Peter the Great. There too, in December, 1825 discontented aristocratic army officers had tried unsuccessfully to force a liberal constitution on autocratic Russia. Also in Senate Square was the former office of the Holy Synod, a department of the tsarist government charged with the administration of the Orthodox Church and religious affairs generally. From this building, in the generation before the revolution of 1905, the Over Procurator, K. P. Pobyedonostsev, had conducted his campaigns against religious dissidents. Restrictions, repression, arrests, exile and imprisonment were combined in an attempt to actualize Pobyedonostsev's view that: "There are not, and must not be any *Russian* Baptists!"

Strolling through the parks and stopping to talk to various people had also been enjoyable. Leningraders are fiercely proud of their beautiful city. Speaking what is generally recognized as the very best Russian, they are always eager to talk, give directions to well-known tourist attractions or suggest visits to less well-known ones. They would heartily second the view of an emigré Leningrader who once told me, "Ah, Leningrad – now that is a *city*! Moscow? – nothing but a wild, overgrown village!"

While resting on a park bench, Lil had been approached by a couple of American women, who announced that they had seen her in the church on Poklonaia Gora on Sunday. Introductions completed, they went on to ask if Lil were a Christian – a real one, who had personally accepted Christ as Lord and Saviour? Mutually satisfied that they were one in Christ, the three of them had gone on to share their experiences in the USSR.

The two Americans had started out as three, determined to do something personally to remedy the lack of Christian literature in the USSR. Their bags full of such literature, they had arrived at the airport. The missing one had been searched and ordered to leave the USSR immediately. These two had miraculously been bypassed in the customs search. They had spent several days walking through Leningrad, dropping their Russian-language tracts into people's mailslots. A shopping bag full of this literature remained, along with some cassette-tape messages, including one especially suitable for presenting the Christian message to Soviet Jews. There was also a book for a particular Russian Christian, complete with name and address. Could Lil make use of this literature, since they had to leave the USSR in a matter of hours?

Lil had remembered the eager faces, outstretched hands and expectant voices of people asking if we had brought them any "gifts". What were our fifteen Russian New Testaments among so many hungry souls? Now in that very ordinary shopping bag there was at least some spiritual food for hundreds. After prayer and farewell embraces, they had parted, praising the sovereign God

who had arranged this "chance" meeting of three unac-
quainted foreigners in a Soviet city of four million.

Our hotel room quite probably had a listening device or
two planted somewhere, but for twenty-five years we had
always shared our day's experiences freely. It was difficult
to keep remembering that this was the USSR, not Canada.
We did not automatically think of turning on the taps and
conversing in the bathroom. Perhaps Lil's report of the
literature transfer should have waited until we were out on
the street.

Fortunately, however, we were never questioned about
that literature, given out over the next two months in
many interesting ways.

4: *The Underground Church?*

Our young translator friend, Adam, had been helpful, if critical. Yes, he was very much aware that there were divisions among the Baptists in the USSR generally and also right here in Leningrad. Admittedly the Reformers had some legitimate grievances, but these could have been worked out within the existing Union of Evangelical Christians-Baptists. Here in Leningrad there were two non-Union churches – unregistered, of course – in the suburbs, one of which he had personally visited and to which he could give us directions. The other, though considerably closer, might be difficult to find, but Brother Mikhail, standing over by the pulpit, would be able to help us.

"Yes," said that brother in response to our questions about the location of that church, "I could give you directions, but I can do better than that. Brother Anton, who is sitting over there by the door, is one of the preachers in that church. Would you like me to introduce you to him?"

A round, beaming face topped with an unruly shock of sandy hair. A burly frame and a crushing handshake, combined with a surprising gentleness and a naturally gracious manner. These were our initial impressions of the man who would become our closest friend during the Leningrad phase of our visit. On hearing that I was both a professor and a pastor, he asked if I had already spoken here. My negative answer puzzled him, especially after I informed him that we had attended several services. He listened attentively to our account of how some of the sisters had been insisting that I speak, or at least bring greetings. Unfortunately, the preaching brother approached on the matter had still not acted on his less-than-enthusiastic, "Yes, that would be very nice." We had read Western press reports of a tightening of controls on participation by visitors, especially those not part of official delegations. Remembering these, and wanting to avoid embarrassing church officials, I had not pursued the question.

"Yes," I concluded, "in 1971, on a weekend visit, I was immediately asked to bring greetings, but this time it has been quite different. Perhaps under present conditions it is not permissible for me to speak?"

"How 'not permitted'?" Anton replied. "It is just a matter of my presenting you to the brethren here. When we first left this church back in the 'sixties, for a while there were absolutely no contacts. Those who stayed felt strongly that needed changes could be made within the existing system, and those of us who left felt just as strongly that we had to form a separate congregation. After several years of painful experiences and rigid separation, we have begun to visit and participate in one another's services. Come to the church office with me and I'll set things up for you to speak tonight, if you wish."

"Greetings, brethren," Anton announced cheerfully as we entered the office. "This is a Christian brother from Canada, who is both a professor and a Baptist pastor. Who is directing the service this evening?"

"I am," replied my one-time dinner partner, he of the *Globe and Mail* old wives' tales. "What can I do for you?" To Anton's suggestion that I should be invited to preach, or at least to bring greetings, he responded with a rather curt, "Unfortunately, not possible. Tonight's program is very full."

Assuring Anton and the assembled brethren that this was fine, and that there would undoubtedly be other occasions, I returned to the sanctuary. As usual, the service was a blessing. Powerful congregational singing, in striking contrast to the polite peepings in many Western churches, encouraged me to sing out lustily. Unlike the usual situation in Canada, mine was not the one voice being heard above all others. Though not previously scheduled as part of the evening's "very full program", Anton's own message was somehow squeezed in and proved to be the high point of the service.

We were delighted to accept Anton's invitation to drive over to his apartment after the service for a cup of tea. Our animated conversation ranged over national, social, church and family topics, but Anton seemed to be bothered by something, as evidenced by his occasionally distracted manner.

"Maybe I shouldn't say anything," he finally blurted out, "but there was quite a conversation after you left the office. Several of the brethren wanted you to preach, declaring that state restrictions must not be allowed to prevent this. 'We ought to obey God, rather than men', you know. But the chairman insisted that only members of official delegations could be permitted to speak. He argued that one had to be especially wary of individual visitors, adding that someone had seen you at an unspecified, but presumably hostile meeting in Geneva." Anton concluded, turning into the apartment block parking lot.

I assured him that I had never attended any kind of meeting in Geneva and we exchanged jokingly-sorrowful comments on the incident as we entered the twelve-year-old apartment block. Its rather run-down exterior suggested a considerably older building, and the wheezy elevator, with its dirty floor and pervasive smell of urine did nothing to improve our impressions.

The apartment was completely different – small, but very clean; tastefully decorated and warmed by the presence of Anton's wife, Vera and eleven-year-old son, Alyosha. An energetic, healthily-attractive woman in her mid-forties, Vera welcomed us enthusiastically and immediately put the kettle on for tea. We settled down in the living-dining room that doubled as a bedroom. The bright-eyed youngster followed our conversation attentively, chomping delightedly on the chewing gum which we offered him.

"He's a real blessing to us," Vera commented, bringing in the tea, "especially because of the way in which he loves to go to church, sing with the young people and play his accordion."

"And there's our daughter, Inessa" Anton interjected, as a very pretty, if somewhat sulky-looking teenager entered the room. We talked for a few minutes and she withdrew to another room, closing the door behind her. Pressed by her peers and the overwhelming influence of the materialist-atheist system, Inessa had been rebelling against the faith and practice of her parents and their church circle. Our general appreciation of the parental heartcry accompanying the prayer, "O Lord, save our children," had suddenly become very specific.

Of course, not all Soviet parents would appreciate this concern for their children's salvation. Anton told us of the experience of a young fellow-churchmember, Vasya. His previous life had been one of violence, drunkenness and general anti-social behaviour – hooliganism, in the common Soviet expression. Yet when he told his mother that he had become a Christian, she was enraged. Apparently, the dramatic change in behaviour meant little to her in comparison with the spiritual separation and the fear of official repression.

She tried every kind of appeal – the foolishness of belief

in God, the prospect of social and government opposition, the risk of losing jobs and apartment, her own very negative feelings. All was in vain. He would not abandon his new-found faith or the fellowship of believers. Concluding that her son had experienced some form of mental collapse, the frantic mother had him committed to a psychiatric institution.

The doctors worked on him for a month, administering chemical and electro-therapy and conducting prolonged counselling sessions. Professional methods, however, met with no more success than parental ones, as the young man persisted in his "religious delusions". He was discharged, but compelled to carry an official document identifying him as a psychopath. As such, he would be unable to obtain a job or an apartment, but the church family had been marvellously supportive, both spiritually and materially. Through it all, Brother Vasya's vibrant testimony had been a great encouragement to many.

"Yes," Anton continued, holding out his cup for more tea, "the church members could sympathize, since all of us have had to face opposition because of our faith. As I was telling you earlier, a group of about thirty to forty of us left the Union Church in the early 'sixties. We could not agree with the position taken by the leadership on such matters as centralizing authority and limiting both evangelism and the Christian education of our children. Under pressure from the authorities, the All-Union Council of Evangelical Christians-Baptists had sent out a letter of instruction and proposed constitutional revisions which would officially implement these unacceptable changes. Well, after much prayer and discussion, we concluded that the leadership at Poklonaia Gora had rendered more to Caesar than they should have, biblically. They would not change and we could not stay; thus, we began to meet separately, endeavoring to conduct our worship according to the Word of God and independent of both the ECB church and meddling state authorities. As it turned out, bowing to state pressure did not ensure that the Poklonaia Gora church would be left at peace. There too the authorities have sought means by which they might limit or prevent the free preaching of the Gospel. "Of course," he concluded, "they have not had to face anything like the pressures which we have experienced."

Our original picture of the church-state relationship with respect to Union and Reform Baptist communities was thus being filled out with some modifying details. The Reformers had been the overwhelming majority of the approximately one thousand Baptists imprisoned during the 1960s. On the other hand, churches belonging to the original Union must have been well-represented among the 2,000+ which were closed during Khrushchev's anti-religious campaign (1959–64), since the Reformers' Union of Churches of Evangelical Christians-Baptists had not been founded until 1965. It had been one of Khrushchev's boasts, incidentally, that the last Christian in the USSR would be displayed – in the manner of a museum curio – on Soviet television in 1965.

One wonders how the late Nikita Khrushchev would have reacted to the sight of some 4,000 Baptist young people gathering for an annual rally in May, 1978 in Khar'kov, in the Ukraine. Signs at the Khar'kov railway stations and in the streets gave directions to the services, prolonged over 13 hours without disturbance from the authorities. Similar meetings were planned for the cities of Rostov and Krasnodar at about the same time. Khrushchev would most likely have been pleased, however, with the actual outcome of these latter two meetings. As the various groups began to arrive in Rostov and Krasnodar, they were met by police squads. Several, including the talented preacher Josif Bondarenko, were arrested and jailed. Others were loaded into vans and police cars and sent back to their home cities under escort. Interestingly enough, all three services had been organized by young people from churches belonging to the old Union. Our previously rather simplistic picture of the Russian Baptists was becoming ever more complicated, and there was more to come.

"Yes," Anton continued, "the Khrushchev years were hard for believers. When we began our separate services back in the early 'sixties, we experienced severe persecution. All society was stirred up against us. The militia and the *druzhnikii* (volunteer civilian police assistants) perpetrated all sorts of cruelties. Whole families were charged. Meetings were disturbed. Sometimes the militia and the *druzhnikii* stood at the door, not permitting anyone to enter the home where we were holding our services. They would even seize people coming out of buses and take them to the police station. Many times we had to hold our meetings out in the streets.

"On one occasion, the militia representatives of the regional soviet's executive committee came to a service and announced that they would not permit anyone to leave until all names had been recorded and all documents checked. Since the authorities already knew us well from many previous interrogations, we refused to give our names or show our documents. The officials then closed us up in the room, not permitting anyone to leave all day – even to relieve himself. Those who arrived for the evening service were not permitted to enter, but were taken to the police station. Around midnight we sang and prayed, then arranged ourselves on the floor to sleep as best we could. One of our guards 'phoned police headquarters, informing them that 'The Baptists are lying down to sleep. What do we do now?' Apparently they were given permission to leave us at that point, for we heard them get into their cars and drive away.

"Our brother, in whose home we met for services, appealed to the authorities to cease their oppression against believers and against his own family. They demanded that he stop permitting these services to be held in his home. He refused and they fined him repeatedly. Fines were endless in those days. Before his arrest, he was fined seven times at 50 rubles each time (about three months' wages in all). Sentenced to a three-year term, he was released after 18 months, thanks to the amnesty commemorating the 50th anniversary of the Bolshevik Revolution of 1917. Services continued in his home and so did the fines – another 13 fines of 50 rubles each.

"Petitions were in vain and actually seemed to increase persecution. Meetings were broken up; believers were arrested and taken to the police station; a number of our brethren were sentenced to two and one-half to three years in prison camps. On one occasion, a believer was able to take a picture of the militia harassing us. Somehow this picture appeared in a Finnish newspaper with the caption: 'The authorities' response to my petition asking them to stop the persecution of believers meeting in my home'."

"Clearly, then," I interjected, "Khrushchev's successors did not repudiate all of his policies. Do you mean that this sort of thing was going on while I was on my first visit to Leningrad in 1971? I attended a couple of services in the Poklonaia Gora church and no one gave any indication of trouble. While I would have liked to meet with the brethren in the unregistered church, I did not know where to find them. Also, I thought that having foreigners visit your services would result in additional repression from the authorities."

"Exactly the reverse," Anton and Vera blurted out in chorus. "The more publicity, the more that foreigners are aware of our churches, the more careful will the authorities have to be. For example, it was precisely in 1971 (May 24) that William Tolbert, President of the Baptist World Alliance was visiting Leningrad. A big banquet in his honor was held in the Poklonaia Gora church. On that very day we had planned to hold our regular service in our brother's home, but both the meeting place and the nearby bus stop were cordoned off by the militia and the *druzhinikii*. They detained everyone, believers and unbelievers alike, at the bus stop. Unbelievers were permitted to proceed; believers were taken off to various police stations.

"The same thing happened at our regular meeting place. Surrounded by militia and *druzhinikii*, about 100 of us dropped to our knees. We prayed and then began to sing: 'nearer my God to Thee, nearer to Thee, E'en though it be a cross that raiseth me'. And we, like those arrested at the bus stop, were taken to the police stations where we were photographed, had our documents verified, and endured all sorts of cruelties. Thus, on that Lord's Day when Tolbert was being honored in the Poklonaia Gora church, we spent the entire day in police stations."

"Apparently something similar happened during Tolbert's visit to Moscow as well," I remarked, remembering a news item which I had read in a Western Christian publication. "While the president of the Baptist World Alliance was being honored in the church on Malovuzovskii Pereulok, a 70-year-old Baptist pastor was dying in a nearby Soviet prison. But is this kind of repression still going on? I understood that the Helsinki Agreement (1975) on European Security and Co-operation did make at least some difference."

"Yes and no," Anton replied. "The Helsinki Agreement, along with various Western human rights and Christian organizations' petitions and protests, have occasionally helped us. Our authorities, concerned to some extent with world public opinion, were moved to act a little more discreetly. But, as you know, the Soviet government insists that the agreements entered into at Helsinki must be interpreted according to each nation's own law code and constitution. And that gives them all the excuse they need.

"One of the worst cases of persecution took place on November 7, 1976 at Petrozavodsk. We were conducting our harvest festival services, an annual celebration at which the brethren throughout our land gather to thank God for the bountiful harvest which He has sent. Many unbelievers also attended the services, held in a brother's house. In the midst of the service, the militia and the *druzhinikii* burst into the room and began a veritable *pogrom* (originally, outbursts of anti-Semitic violence in tsarist Russia). They grabbed believers, twisting their arms and pulling their hair. Chairs and tables were overturned; musical instruments, brought to praise God, were smashed. A cassette tape recorder fell under one of the chairs and kept running. It's all on this tape," he continued, pointing to a nearby bookcase, "children crying, parents trying to calm them, chairs and instruments crashing to the floor, shrieks and curses."

"And now?" I prompted, nodding my acceptance as Vera offered yet another cup of tea.

"Well, the harsh repressive measures have largely ceased. The authorities now talk more tactfully to us and do not disturb our service. But abuses, threats and fines do recur from time to time. In the Leningrad suburb of Kuzmolovo, for example, the brother in whose home services are held does not receive the wages due to him from his job. Our Gorelovo church has been fined for having messy surroundings – merely an excuse, for the fine was obviously for holding services. There have been threats to jail the owner of our building and to stop our services. Once they even threatened to bulldoze the building."

"We've heard of two cases, one in Central Asia and one in Siberia, where the threat became a reality," I commented. The incident in Siberia was especially striking. After prolonged petitioning, the believers finally received official permission to build. They gave sacrificially of both money and labor and constructed a beautiful church building. Within days of completion, the church was bulldozed.

Anton nodded, agreeing with our observation that there seemed to be a deliberate attempt to keep people off-balance by unpredictable, arbitrary behavior. "Yes," he sighed, "experience has shown that even when things seem to be going fairly peacefully, there is no guarantee that harsh measures will not be used again.

"The latest development is that the officials now come to us and say that while they find nothing wrong with our services, we should register our congregation. I should point out that this matter of registration is an open question among the brethren. It does involve extensive reporting on members and financial matters and it does impose certain restrictions on preaching, evangelism, and the Christian education of children and young people. Some of the brethren, however, feel that they can function biblically within these regulations and so they seek registration and the greater measure of security which that seems to provide. But when we asked the officials if the laws under which we were persecuted are still the laws associated with registration they were very embarrassed. 'Yes', they said, 'the same laws are still in effect – but we don't enforce them anymore!' Needless to say," he chuckled, "under those circumstances, we are not going to rush into registration."

Reluctantly, we got up to leave. Anton offered to drive us back to our hotel. Remembering our trip from church we thanked him, but suggested we could go by subway. It was only a short ride, very comfortable, and the combined fare of 10 kopecks (16c) was much less than the cost of the *benzine* (gasoline) which his Zaporozhets would burn.

"No, we cannot permit that," he insisted, "it's out of the question. After all, the Lord has provided us with a car and I would not think of letting our honored guests take the subway. Come, Vera, you may as well go along for the ride."

And so we crammed ourselves into his little Zaporozhets, scarcely larger than a good-sized packing crate. The now-familiar puffs of smoke and pungent gas-oil odor combined effectively with the lurching of a semi-apopleptic transmission and the yo-yo motion of a short-wheelbase car rapidly crossing innumerable raised tram tracks. In no time at all, my rapidly-churning stomach was blending in an interesting off-beat counter-gurgle with the syncopated roaring of the motor.

Mercifully, we had arrived at our hotel. I got out without the aid of a shoehorn, but needed a bit of help from Lil in negotiating the peculiarly rotating sidewalk. I muttered a rather strained thanks for the ride. Hoping that my pale green face would be interpreted as a reflection from the hotel's doorway lights, we proceeded gratefully to the relative quietness and stability of our room.

5: *And They Brought Unto Him Children*

"I saw you at church the other day," said an attractive young man as he came over to our table in the hotel dining room. "Where are you from – America?"

Introductions completed, we began to discuss different aspects of Christian life in our two countries, including the raising of children. We knew that it must be difficult, given the basic hostility of the Soviet régime toward religion. The state works diligently to promote atheism, making use of day-care centres and nursery schools, the almost-compulsory child and youth organizations (Octobrists, Pioneers, Komsomol), the mass media, and the entire educational system. How do Christian parents such as himself cope with the problem?

Our young friend began: "It is indeed difficult. Some Christian parents have even had their children taken away from them to be raised in boarding schools. But this kind of pressure simply welds the believers more closely together. There are many of us young couples with small children, in the Leningrad church. Though the state officially prohibits public religious instruction of minors, recently it has become somewhat safer to take our children to the regular preaching services. In addition, we have frequent private discussions with the preaching brethren and get together in our homes. There we encourage one another, pray together, and discuss ways to overcome the problems we face.

"And our numbers are growing. Over the past few years

especially, some of our fellow-workers have begun to ask us questions about why we seem so different in attitude and life-style from most other Soviet citizens. Knowing that at one time many of us had been as bad as the worst of them, they also wonder what has made such an amazing change in our lives. We answer their questions simply by telling them about Christ. Of course we are very careful not to take work time for these discussions. God gives us plenty of opportunities, as we meet with these questioners during slack periods, lunch breaks, or while waiting for trams. Some of the questioners have mocked us, others quickly lost interest. But a few of them have even come to our homes to meet and talk with our Christian friends. And it was not long before a number of them became believers, accepted baptism and joined the church."

We shook hands warmly as he returned to the hotel's kitchen where he worked. The meal itself had not been too inspiring – a very limited menu, snail-like service, rather unappetizing food, and a very loud Soviet band trying to play American jazz. But the unexpected Christian-fellow-ship "dessert" made up for the meal's shortcomings.

The abstract, general problem of Christian child-raising in the Soviet Union was rapidly being shifted to the plane of the concrete and practical, thanks to our meetings with Anton and Vera and with this young man. And that change in focus had been accompanied by a profound spiritual and emotional impact. It was one thing to read, for example, that in 1975 a petition bearing 1,147 signatures had been presented to the Soviet authorities, protesting against the removal of children from their Christian parents. It was quite another matter to listen to the story of one such child as it was told to me by a relative in Canada.

He was ten years old, his widowed mother's only child and he had been taken away from her. The boarding school was hundreds of kilometres away from his home and the mother was strictly forbidden to visit her son. Days stretched into months before she received a letter. The boy reported that the teachers constantly ridiculed Christianity and harassed him repeatedly in the classroom. In the dormitories classmates made him the butt of crude jokes, tormenting him verbally and even physically. He concluded the smuggled-out letter with these words: "But at night, dear Mama, when the lights are out, I crawl under my bed and I pray."

A year later, a second letter arrived. Its general tone was much like the first, but the anxious mother shed a joyful tear as she read the concluding sentence: "Now, dearest Mama, at night when the lights are out, there are two of us under the bed praying."

Another year passed and a third letter arrived. Classroom conditions had not really changed, though the boy expressed relatively little concern about them. The letter ended on this triumphant note: "Dearest Mama, now we don't even bother to put out the lights, because most of the boys in the dormitory are praying."

A few days later we had a unique opportunity to see home and church working together to strengthen Christian children's knowledge and convictions for the daily battle with atheism. We had spent a few hours with Vanya, a lanky, red-bearded tenor in the Poklonaia Gora choir and his wife, Elena, a plump, jovial accountant. They spoke enthusiastically about their complementary witness at the factory where they both worked, she in the office and he in the engineering department. Our comments on the omnipresent slogans: "Hail the victorious Communist Party!", "Forward in the struggle to fulfil the tenth five-year Plan!" – were met with a polite question.

"And what kind of slogans would one see in your country?"

We laughed together as we tried, in clumsy Russian, to explain the difference between permanent political slogans and permanent commercial appeals to buy this, that, or the other product. We wept together as we visited the Piskarevskoe cemetery and museum, honoring the approximately 1.5 million who died in the 1,000-day siege of Leningrad during the Second World War.

After the evening service, Vanya asked if we would like a ride back to our hotel, adding that we could either go directly or first pick up their daughter, who had been attending a friend's birthday party. Delighted with this unexpected opportunity, we chose the latter. A few minutes later we pulled into an open space behind one of several four-storey concrete apartment blocks.

"Best not to say anything; just walk along behind us," Vanya advised. "People here are not used to seeing foreigners coming to visit, and one never knows what they will say about it – and to whom."

The apartment was crowded with about 30 people, a few adults and the rest a colorful jumble of bright-eyed, neatly-dressed children, aged 10 to 15. Vanya introduced us to our hostess, a slender, thirtyish woman whose grey eyes still reflected the sorrow of the sudden death of her young pastor-husband. She insisted that we share in the birthday lunch, and we were quickly ushered into the dining room.

It was an amazing sight. We had seen the meats available in Leningrad shops. Those weirdly-shaped chunks of flesh looked as if they had been casually hacked from the carcass, or perhaps simply gathered up after the unfortunate animal had been hit by a train. Now, after hours of queue-standing and some mysterious kitchen magic, our hostess had transformed that meat into juicy cutlets, delicate head-cheese and savoury stews. The dazzling array of baked goods, especially the flaky, cream-filled pastries, was even more impressive.

Among the parents who had come to collect their children was a sturdy forty-year-old worker. We had been left alone at the table for a few minutes. Leaning over my shoulder and speaking very softly he asked if I would like a copy of a recently-printed booklet which the brethren had produced. It was the memoirs of the widow of a Baptist pastor from Riga, in Latvia, martyred during the takeover of his country by the USSR during World War II. I replied in an equally low voice that this would be a highly-prized item and that I was honored by this expression of trust. He got up to leave, promising to deliver the *samizdat* (self-published) booklet at the next service.

Shortly afterwards Lil returned with Vanya and Elena, asking if I was ready to leave. As we walked along the corridor, we met one of the preaching brethren from the church, the one with whom I had begun a discussion about Sunday Schools. Smiling warmly, he gave a quick look around and motioned us to follow him out into the backyard.

"You remember asking me about how we supplement home training?" he asked, after we were safely outside. "Well," he continued, "you have just been present at one of our Sunday School sessions. Among our 3,000 members there are, of course, many with young children. Those many children have birthdays scattered throughout the entire year. They have their parties, inviting friends from other families. Somehow, it generally happens that one of us preaching brethren has a child or a grandchild invited to the party and so we also drop in. We may lead them in some games, Bible quizzes, hymns, tell them a story or two. And so we have these, what you might call Sunday Schools, in various parts of the city. Of course," he sighed, "sometimes the authorities become aware of what we are actually doing and then there is trouble. A brother has recently been arrested for permitting one of these Sunday Schools to be held in his home. But we will keep on."

It was both humbling and saddening. These Christians were determined, at whatever cost, to train up their children in the way they should go. We thought about our North American evangelical Sunday Schools with all their advantages, wondering how many of them could really match this utter seriousness of purpose. Our friend smiled as we told him about the late Brother Timchenko, an aged Baptist pastor from the USSR whom we had met during his visit to Canada. We had asked about how Russian Baptists managed the Christian education of their children, given the prohibition of Sunday Schools. The white-moustached old man had looked me full in the face and replied simply: "We teach them in the home. Don't you?"

All things considered, we thought that, as compared with most Christians in the West, Christians in the USSR do a more effective job of Christian education. Officially, they cannot have Sunday Schools and they certainly cannot establish Christian day schools. In the West, children from Christian homes certainly face peer pressure and the influence of humanist-oriented teachers, committed in varying degrees to changing their students' beliefs. But these students do not have to face the persistent, systematic atheist indoctrination that is the daily lot of Christian children in the Soviet educational system. In the USSR, some of the children from Christian homes have been won away from the faith, but it is by no means clear that this is more extensive than among Christians in the West, with all their advantages. In fact, judging from some of the stories which we heard, the reverse might well be true.

One fourth-grade youngster, regularly harassed by her

atheist science teacher, maintained a sweet disposition and refused to be drawn into an argument. One day the teacher was expounding the accomplishments of the Soviet cosmonauts, concluding with the triumphant announcement: "Our cosmonauts thus travelled hundreds of thousands of kilometres in space and found absolutely no evidence of any 'god' there." Turning to the Christian student, the teacher asked sarcastically, "Well, Tanya, don't you think that if, after all that space travel, our cosmonauts did not see 'God', it is proof that no such 'God' exists?"

"I don't know about that," Tanya replied politely, "but I do know that only the pure in heart can see God at all."

A few days later we were discussing the matter of school problems with Anton. It was yet another surprise to discover that even in the USSR it was sometimes possible for a determined parent to "fight city hall" in defense of his children.

"Our children had also been experiencing various kinds of discrimination and harassment," Anton observed, as we sat parked in his Zaporozhets on the riverbank near the Winter Palace. "Not wanting to be unprepared, I carefully noted the specific times and nature of these incidents. I also investigated the relevant sections of the constitution and the laws and regulations pertaining to educational matters. It was only after I had done this that I arranged for an interview with the principal of the school."

I nodded, observing that this seemed to tally with what I had read about the documents circulated by persecuted believers in the USSR. First, they simply asked for scrupulous adherence to existing Soviet laws guaranteeing basic human rights and fundamental freedoms. Second, they were always completely accurate and thoroughly documented. For example, one well-known Western research organization, specializing in the question of religion in the USSR, noted that no errors of fact could be found in a mass of documents circulated by Russian Christians over a 12-year period.

"I found the principal somewhat defensive, almost hostile," Anton continued, "but not wishing to jeopardize my case, I refrained from answering in the same way. Instead, I simply presented the facts, referring to various rights and privileges apparently guaranteed by our government. Politely, I requested that he take appropriate steps to remedy the situation and then I left."

His eyes twinkling with merriment, he concluded his account, "The next day I received a phone call from some higher educational official. He demanded to know what I had done, since the whole school was in an uproar. Briefly, I reviewed the whole affair, making pointed references to constitutionally-guaranteed rights and privileges. Dumbfounded, he grudgingly agreed with my position and promised remedial action. After that incident, our children were left in peace. You know, the whole affair proved to me that the teachers themselves do not know the rules under which they are supposed to be operating. Also, sometimes at least, we are able to get redress by appealing to the constitution and other documents. Admittedly, this may be the exception, rather than the rule."

It was only a few weeks later, in Kiev, that we came face to face with "the rule". The daughter of a prominent religious dissident, an attractive teenager, had been the top student in her high school and was expected to win the gold medal for scholarship. Only one thing stood between her and entry to the university on a handsome fellowship, with the promise of a brilliant academic or professional career to follow. She was to write a competitive essay on the subject, "The Place of Lenin in my Heart".

The temptation to write the expected kind of essay was very strong, but her Christian convictions held firm. In the introduction to her essay she stated simply that she was a born-again believer in Jesus Christ. As such, He alone filled her heart, occupying a place that no one else, however great, could fill.

Needless to say, she received neither the gold medal nor the university fellowship. Denied access to the university, she took a job as a parcel clerk in the post office. Six thousand bright Baptist young people in a 30-year period after the Second World War had gone through essentially similar experiences.

Sasha had been more fortunate than most. He had actually graduated as an economist from the University of Leningrad. When we first met, he had insisted on practising his very good English on us, asking anxiously about his accent.

"Very, very good," Lil and I answer in chorus, adding that he sounded as if he could pass for a native on Oxford Street in London.

A look of mild displeasure crossed his face as he replied in BBC English, "Oh, that's too bad. I want to sound like an American!"

We were interested to learn that he had been working at a Leningrad bank for the past two years, noting the slight emphasis on the word *had*. Despite good reports from his superiors and no indication of any dissatisfaction with his work, he had been dismissed just last month. He knew, of course, that the Lord would provide, but the experience had been a very distressing one. Would we pray for him, that his faith might remain firm and that he would be a good witness in his new job? The university graduate in economics was about to become a taxi driver.

6: *"It's a Different System"*
   (or, "Goods Satisfactory, or . . .")

Shopping was an interesting experience which we, unlike most Western tourists, actually shared with ordinary Soviet citizens. Some few food stores offered the range of products, though not the quality of goods available in the average small-town grocery stores in North America. Fresh meat and produce, especially, seemed to be in short supply and of poor quality and only a few of these Soviet "supermarkets" sold bread. In some cases, electric cash registers were replacing the centuries-old abacus. Tradition apparently dies hard, however, since we heard reports that the early users of calculators and computers in the USSR had occasionally checked their electronic answers by using the abacus.

In order to buy the makings of a simple lunch, I would have to go to several shops. Bread was cheap at 20 kopeks (32¢ Cdn.) for a large loaf, but I would have to go to a separate pastry shop for a few tarts or a slice of torte. The meatshop was always crowded, with people buying fresh meat or poultry at four to six rubles a kilo ($3.00-$4.50/lb.) I would generally buy smoked sausage – perhaps too greasy for most North Americans – at $2.40 a pound. The wizened, spotted apples were regularly bypassed even by produce-starved Soviet citizens, who preferred the imported oranges at an incredible 40 kopeks (64¢) each. Enterprising rural shoppers, planning to sell these oranges at a profit to their fellow-villagers, bought them by the half-bushel.

In each shop I would have to stand in line three times. In the first, I would pick out the specific item, with the clerk weighing out the requested quantity. Then I would queue up at the single cashier's kiosk to obtain a ticket for that purchase. Clutching this slip of paper I would return to the first line-up to pick up my purchase. Thus, if we wanted to eat supper at 6:00, I generally started shopping at 4:00.

Despite considerable improvements during the Khrushchev and Brezhnev years, consumer goods are still in short supply. Though of generally unattractive design and poor quality, these goods are nevertheless rather expensive. It would take a month's wages, for example, to buy either a man's suit or a woman's light summer coat. A week's wages would buy a pair of shoes, made of a plastic-like material; or a woman's sweater, though the more attractive sweaters would cost about twice as much. Those wanting a small electric washing machine, shaped like a gas barrel and with hand-operated wringer, would have to spend almost two months' wages. A refrigerator about the size of a large trunk would cost three months' wages.

Soviet citizens are constantly on the alert for quality goods, which are rarely available and then only in limited quantities. An oft-repeated Soviet joke begins with the report of a large poster in the department store window. At the top is the boldprint announcement: "Attention citizens! We have received a shipment of 10,000 ladies' coats from Czechoslovakia." In much smaller letters, readers are informed that 9,500 coats have been reserved for government officials, economic administrators and military officers. As usual, 498 coats will have been appropriated by department store employees. Then again, in large print: "Citizens may form a queue at counter 26 at 9:00 a.m. to purchase these coats."

Surly clerks, earning from one-half to two-thirds of the average monthly wage, are not especially anxious to please, or even to serve, for that matter. Some of them supplement their meagre wages by taking bribes to put away desirable goods for special customers. Others resort to outright theft. On an early-morning visit to one of Leningrad's museums, for example, we noticed a number of untypically happy-looking attendants bustling along with two-foot sausages tucked under their arms. One evening, while passing a large restaurant, we were surprised to see a sign on the door announcing *Mesto nyet!* (No room!) Puzzled, since three-quarters of the tables were unoccupied, we asked the doorman about it.

"It's because of what's going on in the kitchen," he replied, with a meaningful wink. Then, since we still looked a bit blank, he grunted, "To speak plainly, the help is stealing the food."

Western goods are highly-prized. The ordinary plastic shopping bag, depending on the kind of label on it, will bring from five to ten rubles ($8–10). One night, half-asleep in our hotel room, we were awakened by a hesitant knock on the door. There stood a fat, rather greasy-looking man, his black eyes darting nervously up and down the corridor. He first addressed me in German. Then in response to my "Pardon?", he switched to broken English. Did we want to sell anything – clothes, shoes, cameras?

Walking along Nevsky Prospekt one day, I was met by a young man who announced that he wanted to buy my necktie and sunglasses, then and there. I smiled as I walked on, remembering the experience of a Canadian student. A fashion-conscious Soviet youth had offered the Canadian 150 rubles ($240) for his bluejeans – then and there on the street.

We had brought two used paperback novels with us.

Perhaps a Soviet bookstore would be willing to purchase them. At any rate, the experience of trying it might prove interesting. Reluctantly, I headed for the library while Lil, passport in hand, went off to the bookstore.

The clerk was polite, but puzzled at Lil's question, part of our personal survey of Soviet bookstores. "A Bible? No, we don't have that book. Pushkin's fairy stories?" Again a negative response. "You wish to sell us some English-language books? Yes, that might be possible, but you will have to ask the manager."

Ushered into a back room, Lil waited while the manageress, a briskly-efficient woman in her forties, finished talking to a customer. She examined the books and the passport and then announced the price which she was willing to pay. Her tone indicated a non-negotiable, "take it or leave it" position. We had bought the books at a local grocery store back home at 25¢ each. She offered Lil five rubles for the better-quality book, four rubles for the one almost falling apart. That worked out to just over $14 at the official exchange rate.

Quality goods are available in the Soviet Union, but these are to be found only in shops reserved for the élite or for tourists, who will pay for these goods in hard currency. Thus, it gave us a kind of perverse pleasure to take our needy Christian friends into the *Beriozka* shops. As we entered, we would smile pleasantly at the irate managers who obviously resented our giving ordinary Soviet citizens access to this restricted territory.

We planned to buy a couple of cassette tape recorders, preferably of German or Japanese manufacture. For some years, Anton and Vera had been recording Christian short-wave broadcasts from the West. Better quality equipment would make for clearer cassette-tape messages, useful for evangelism and Christian education.

At first our wide-eyed Russian friends just stood there

in the middle of what was to them a shopper's paradise. Apart from the obvious difference in quality, variety and abundance of goods, the whole atmosphere was different from that in regular department stores. There were no queues. The clerks were amazingly helpful. They would cheerfully show you numerous items and let you handle them. Instead of becoming angry when you decided not to buy, these amazing clerks kept smiling. Their smiles, Lil and I thought, seemed a bit strained, less natural than those they wore when we appeared unaccompanied by our Soviet friends.

Savoring the delicious experience, Anton and Vera carefully chose a couple of watches, some scarves, and an elegant-looking fur hat. These items would be re-sold at several times their cost, with the profit used to help distressed Christians or support various aspects of the church's ministry. Unfortunately, neither of the two shops visited had foreign-made tape recorders and we had to settle for two Soviet machines.

When we met a day or two later, Anton reported that one machine was fine but the other was defective. The volume control did not work, there was no transcription cord, and the guarantee card was also missing. Somewhat apologetically, he asked if we could return this example of Soviet quality control and either get a working model or a cash refund. I agreed readily, puzzled by his rather worried look. It would be a simple matter to correct the problem. From which of the two stores had the defective machine come – the second?

Carefully rehearsing our lines beforehand, Lil and I walked confidently into the shop. About ten minutes later, frustrated and angry, we strode out into the street again. Not only had they refused us a replacement or a refund, but the clerk kept insisting that the machine had worked perfectly when she sold it to us. Worse still, in response to our protests, one of the clerks accused us of having sold the cord, lost the card, and wrecked the recorder.

Anton wondered aloud whether the recorder had been bought, after all, in the *first* store. Much less enthusiastically I agreed to try again. Anton would wait outside the store, while Lil and Vera stayed in the car.

Shuffling diffidently up to the counter, I asked a familiar-looking clerk if I could please return this tape recorder which we had bought there a couple of days ago. Tests, a succession of supervisors' decisions, 'phone calls all over Leningrad all ended with the same firm answer. Without the missing cord and card, no return.

Some two hours after having entered this second store I walked out on to the street again, still carrying the defective recorder minus cord and card. Anton was more than a little concerned, wondering if I might be already visiting some police station. Our wives were certainly anxious, all the more so because a suspicious-looking, large black car had been parked behind our inconspicuous Zaporozhets.

Explaining the situation as simply as we could, we got into the car, with Anton muttering something about having picked up a tail. Some agile manoeuvering in and out of traffic indicated that there was no one following us.

"Fear sometimes has very big eyes," Vera laughed nervously as we finally parked on a deserted street.

"So now you are stuck with a useless tape recorder?" I asked.

"Well, maybe we can get it fixed somehow," Anton replied, somewhat dubiously; "I'm just sorry that you had to go through all that unpleasantness for nothing. We've wasted the time you could have spent in the library."

"Not at all, not at all," I protested. "My work was proceeding very well and I can afford to take some time off."

"And we've had an experience that very few tourists in the USSR would ever have," Lil added.

"Well, that's certainly true," the two of them laughed.

"Oh, oh," Vera gasped, looking at her watch. "I have just fifteen minutes to get to the dentist's. All the excitement almost made me forget the dreadful experience awaiting me."

"I suppose everyone hates to go to the dentist," Lil observed sympathetically. "I'm grateful that at least our home dentist is very gentle and tries to minimize the pain."

"It's not so much the pain," Vera replied. "The dentist's office is above a fruit shop and what with the swarms of fruit flies, I hate to open my mouth!"

It was a beautiful day, still early in the afternoon. After a quick check of our tourist map, we decided to make the short trip out to Pushkin formerly *Tsarskoe Selo* (Tsar's Village), site of one of the royal palaces, which was now a museum devoted to the life and works of the great Russian writer. Arriving at the appropriate Leningrad railway station, we found our way through the crowds to the ticket machines on the departure platform. I stood there, trying to read the somewhat faded instructions.

"How does one get a ticket?" asked a short forty-ish man sidling up to me. I replied that he, as a native, could undoubtedly solve that problem more readily than I, a confused Canadian tourist. Smiling warmly, he identified himself as a military history professor from Kaliningrad, the westernmost point in the USSR. He was on holiday in Leningrad and was eagerly looking forward to a visit to Pushkin, being a great admirer of "the Russian Shakespeare". In a few minutes, the instructions were deciphered, the appropriate coins inserted, levers pulled. Clutching our three tickets, we boarded the electric train headed for Pushkin, less than an hour away.

On arrival, we walked the short distance from the railway station to the palace, continuing our pleasant conversation and viewing snapshots of one another's children. We chuckled in recognition as we discovered that professor-student relationships in Canada and the USSR have a good deal in common.

As with most tourist attractions in the USSR, the admission price was very low – about 30 cents. We paused for a few moments at the wicket in order to check the large simplified map which indicated the general layout of the extensive grounds and buildings.

"Perhaps we should begin with a stroll through the grounds," Lil suggested, looking at me.

"Sounds like a good idea," our companion remarked. "I've enjoyed our conversation very much. Would you mind if I came along with you?"

We agreed immediately, grateful to have a personal Pushkin guide, so to speak, and for the additional opportunity to present a Christian witness. Conversation shortly got around to that topic once again. As on the train, however, it seemed to be uni-directional. Despite a variety of approaches and topics, his response continued to be that same puzzling blend of polite attentiveness and polite silence. We moved on to other subjects.

Our companion's military-history background and Soviet patriotism were evident in his comments on Nazi destruction of the palace and art treasures during World War II. We were tremendously impressed with the work of restoration. Meticulous research into all the details of architecture, furnishings and decorations had provided a description of the various rooms in the palace. Traditional arts and crafts had been revived, as in the case of the 90-year-old woman whom we saw teaching needlecraft to an attractive teenager. The costs of course, were staggering, with the restoration of one room requiring the expenditure of some three million dollars.

In the course of our sightseeing, Lil and I frequently decided to go in a different direction than was chosen by our unexpected guide. More correctly, we decided initially to go in different directions, but he invariably changed his mind and decided to come with us. Toward the end of the day, he announced that, having come all the way from Kaliningrad and not knowing when he would be able to return, there was one other Pushkin display that he was determined to see.

We had thrilled to deeply-moving recitals of Pushkin's poetry by the attendants at various displays. But it had been a long day, and neither our tired feet nor our culture-stuffed minds could absorb any more.

"Enjoy yourself," we said, extending our hands for a final shake, "but we're simply too tired and so we'll be heading back to Leningrad."

The absolutely essential final visit was reluctantly abandoned – after a pause of about five seconds – and he decided that perhaps, after all, he would return to Leningrad with us. With whom, we wondered, would he be sharing his recollections of the day's activities? Would it be with his wife, children and university colleagues in Kaliningrad – or with the Leningrad branch of the KGB?

7: *"Let Your Light So Shine Before Men"*

We were ready long before nine on that Sunday morning, excited about the prospect of actually meeting with one of the so-called "underground" churches. Popular in the West, this expression was never used by the Soviet believers which we met, not even those who attended services in unregistered congregations. In fact, when I spoke of an underground church, my Russian friend quickly corrected me.

"Do you think that we're a bunch of moles? No, not underground, but rather letting our light so shine among men that they may see our good works and glorify our Father which is in Heaven!" he declared.

Mercifully, my apprehensions about yet another trip in the Zaporozhets proved to be worse than the actual experience. Thus it was with reasonable strength and improving agility that we wriggled our way out of the car and walked up the short path towards the cottage-like building which served as their meeting place.

"By the way," Anton said, as we approached the gate, "we solved the tape-recorder problem. And here is the brother through whom God did it," he added, pointing to a handsome young man with a glowing smile. He was a recently-converted engineer, who just happened to know where to take the recorder to get a satisfactory settlement.

"This brother and sister are visitors from Canada," Anton said to the pastor, a gentle old saint who had spent 15 years in Siberia during the Stalinist terror. One after another they came up to greet us. There were the familiar beaming sisters in their neat skirts and white blouses. Serious-looking men in their thirties, wearing dark "suits" were followed by shy children, giggling delightedly at the peculiar grammatical errors made by this *professor*, if you please! We were glad to see the dozen or so young people with their musical instruments. A young Red Army soldier, a Christian several thousand miles from home, spoke simply, but with great earnestness, telling us how delighted he was to have found this group of believers.

A sturdy octogenarian took my hand and ran it gently over the back of his misshapen skull. "The rest of my head was shot off during the last war," he stated in a matter-of-fact tone.

Apart from the difference in size of the congregation and the physical surroundings, we might have been in the registered Union church. Vigorous congregational singing alternated with brief, urgent messages or musical numbers from the young people. When the pastor announced that the choir would sing, about 25 people – a third of the congregation – moved to the front of the room. If not quite as professional as the Academy Choir of the Poklonaia Gora church, they were still very good. Finally, as elsewhere, the familiar chorus of reverent whispering-praying provided an inspiring, supportive echo to the single voice leading in prayer.

One obvious difference between the two churches was the matter of our participation. A scribbled note was passed to Anton from a member. Could the brother and sister sing for us, in English? And so we sang the Bible-verse chorus, "Seek ye first the Kingdom of God."

"Amen! Heart-felt thanks. Glory to God!" the congregation responded as we finished.

"And now," the pastor announced, "our brother will bring us a few words."

Haltingly, but inspired by the atmosphere of Christian warmth, I told them of my grandfather's ministry of 60+ years and of my dual role as professor of Russian history and pastor of an independent Baptist church. Encouraging expressions of appreciation and provision of the Russian words I could not remember helped me to go on. I was even beginning to enjoy the hand-hidden giggling of children, trying to stifle their chortling over my unique word endings. I think they especially enjoyed my introductory anecdote. As a child, addressing my grandfather on behalf of the family, I had confused two similar-sounding words. Instead of *vnuchkii* (little grand-children), I had greeted him on behalf of his *vonyuchkii* (little skunks!).

The service was over, but no one seemed too anxious to leave. As usual, we stood around talking animatedly to various members of the congregation. In a few minutes, a strong male voice broke through the hum of conversation.

"Brothers and sisters, quiet please! This sister wants to repent and place her faith in Christ as Saviour. Let us gather around and pray with her."

And so it was that we were privileged to witness, in Soviet Russia, the universal miracle of that grace of God which draws lost and helpless sinners to salvation. What made this instance especially thrilling was the fact that the woman in question had visited the services previously in order to mock the believers – and the fact that she was 92 years old.

"Manya, come and meet our friends from Canada," Anton called out to a vivacious brunette in her twenties. I had been struck by the rapt attention with which she had listened to my presentation, despite the stumbling Russian. Anton introduced her and left to talk to someone else, suggesting that we ask her to tell us her story.

"I was born into a Christian family in Moldavia," she began, "and all my brothers and sisters became Christians at an early age. I was different. Year after year, my parents' beliefs and my parents' control became more and more objectionable to me. I felt intolerably bound by them and yearned for the day that I would be free of all that.

"When I began my university studies in chemistry, it was at a city far away from home. Free at last of those Christian restraints which I hated, I listened eagerly to my atheist professors and plunged into every kind of sinful pleasure. Yet I was not happy.

"After graduation, I came to Leningrad. I thought that if learning and indulgence in fleshly pleasure had not brought happiness and a sense of purpose into my life, perhaps meaningful work and new friends would. It was to no avail, however, and if anything, I became even more lonely, sorrowful, and despairing.

"There was a girl in my department, an excellent worker, very friendly and co-operative, but I hated her. She was a believer, and her very presence reminded me, day after day, of my former Christian home life. Worse still, while I was miserable she was settled and happy – and she was always talking about Christ."

Tears trickled down her cheeks as she concluded her story, "I thank God now for that girl's love for me and for her faithful witness. Through her, God brought me to Himself in salvation. As parents you can understand my parents' joy when I asked their forgiveness for my years of rebellion and told them that their prodigal had come home."

As she left to catch the train, we thought of another Manya, whom we had met at the Poklonaia Gora church. A plump pensioner with a radiant, broad Slavic face, she had virtually adopted us as her children, and we always looked forward to seeing her at the services. Our admiration for this simple saint kept growing from week to week as she told us more about her life.

Her pension was very small, forty rubles a month. But

unlike many other pensioners she did not take a part-time job to supplement her meagre income. Instead she lived very simply, careful about every kopek and devoting almost all her time to Christian service.

"Every morning I ask God to direct me to someone, and then I go out, trusting that He will do so. Today, while waiting at a bus stop, I met a young Jewish man, very disturbed because his marriage had just broken up. He listened so attentively as I spoke to him of Christ. On another occasion it will be in the park, in a shop, or on the street. God has never once failed to direct me to someone every day. I just wish I had something printed to leave with them," she sighed, "but you see how few Bibles we have, leave alone other Christian literature."

We dipped into our supply of Russian Christian tracts and gave her a few. With several weeks remaining in our stay and numerous churches to visit, we had to ration our distribution. But we could not refuse the pleadings of a nurse, who worked with terminally-ill patients. Returning to the Poklonaia Gora church at a later date, we saw the same nurse, accompanied by a young man. Judging from his whispered questions, vigorous assenting nods at her answers, and his look of intense concentration, as he stood with eyes rivetted on the preacher, he was not far from the kingdom of God.

"You'll have dinner with us, of course," said Vera cheerfully, breaking into our reverie.

"And that will give you a chance to hear a very interesting account of some of our experiences back in the 'sixties," Anton chimed in. "I have a brother's recollections on tape," he added.

The dinner was simple, but tasty, though Anton grumbled good-naturedly at the shreds of green onion garnishing his bowl of soup. Grass, he called it. Armed with steaming cups of tea we settled down to hear Philip's story, bits and pieces of which had come out in previous conversations.

"I was born into a religious home and was a confirmed member of the church. It was at age twenty-three that my soul was awakened to seek after God, simply to find an answer to the question of whether God really exists. First of all, I found the gospel in my own Finnish language and began to read it extensively in my free time. I had always thought of myself as a religious man, a believer. But as I read the gospel I began to see myself as a lost man, one who had defied the law of the All-Highest God.

"After some time, I found a Baptist fellowship and began to attend its services. I was deeply stirred by the re-born preachers and the living Word of God and became convinced that I was a great sinner. But I suffered for a long time, saying 'I will repent today, or tomorrow'. It seemed that something always held me back. Finally God in His mercy gave me the gift of repentance, enabling me to bow the knee and turn to Him. From that day a great joy filled my heart. A short time later I was baptized and joined the church here in Leningrad.

"There were about 130 of us who were meeting separately from the church on Poklonaia Gora. Having my own home, I was willing to let the brethren meet there and I petitioned the authorities for permission to hold meetings in my home until we could get a regular place of worship. They rejected my petition and continued their earlier persecutions and arrests. We continued to meet in homes – in my home after 1966 – even though our services were regularly broken up by the militia and the *druzhinikii*.

"Eventually the authorities summoned me to come to their offices and face charges. When I did not respond they came to my home early one morning and took me in for questioning. The investigation dragged on for four and one-half months, after which I was arrested under Section 142 of the Criminal Code – violation of the laws on religious cults.

"I must say that I have never had such great joy in my heart – not even at my conversion – as when I was under judicial investigation and then in prison. The Bible tells us not to be fearful when they bring you before governors and magistrates, for God will give you the words and you will speak with wisdom. When I read that I simply cannot express how, from that moment, God gave me such wisdom and strength that they could not stand before it.

"During my imprisonment there were many others awaiting trial: murderers, terrible robbers, violent men. One day, in a line-up with all these men, the police officer had me take two steps forward and turn around. Then, facing these men he declared 'You men are not the *real* criminals.' Then, pointing to me, he almost shouted, 'There is your real criminal!'

"Later, when we were brought into a large room, some of these men asked me the nature of my crimes, since they were such great criminals and I was supposed to be still greater. I told them that I was a great thief who was stealing souls from Satan and winning them to Christ. Thus, I was able to explain the nature of my crimes to the prisoners and to the guards, for they did not understand.

"In each of the many cell blocks in which I was placed there were many terrible criminals. I conversed with all of them, preaching openly in each cell block. Always, from 80-90% of the prisoners listened to the gospel. There were very few who opposed.

"At my trial the judge asked one of the witnesses, a Christian, how he viewed the petition which I had sent to the UN. The witness insisted that before he could give an answer he would like the judge to read the petition, which, incidentally, described the authorities' disruption of our services. The judge replied that it was the business of the witness to answer questions, not to give advice to the court. But the witness refused to answer until the petition had been read and so the matter was dropped.

"The judge asked another witness, also a Christian, what he could say about the accused. I had declared that formerly I was an unbeliever and a drunkard. It was reported that I had become a different person. I agreed with the statement that I had become a completely different person, but why then was I *now* before the court? Pressed by the judge, the witness replied, 'I am also a believer, guilty of the same crimes as the three who sit on the bench under judgment. I will tell you no more about them except that they are my brothers and sisters.

"When arrested, I had with me a Finnish Bible and a Russian New Testament, which they confiscated as they always do when a person is imprisoned. I appealed to the authorities, noting that since the Bible is not a forbidden book it should be returned. The reply to my petition – a scribbled note on a torn piece of paper – was negative. Afterwards, I received a little packet of atheist literature which they wanted me to read, but the Bible and New Testament were not returned.

"I knew that the court would find me guilty and that I would be sent to a prison camp. Greatly desiring to have my Bible, I turned to God in prayer and fasting for five days. Just before I was to be sent to the camp, God answered my prayer and I received both my Bible and New Testament. I was very happy.

"During my stay in camp, hundreds read that Russian New Testament for themselves, while I read my Finnish Bible. I spoke to many about the mighty deeds of Christ, of what He accomplished at Golgotha and by His resurrection. A few of the prisoners would mock and laugh, and that made me very sorrowful. Some would simply leave, but most would listen respectfully to God's Word. It was an exceptionally joyful period in my life.

"Though camp conditions were often very difficult, it is precisely at such times that God is especially near. I learned much and acquired great riches through these trials, sharing somewhat in the sufferings of our Lord Jesus Christ. Though I could not share in His suffering on Golgotha, while I was in the camp I learned to understand more clearly the depth of those sufferings and to value them supremely.

"I thank God for this opportunity to record this material on tape, and I ask you, dear brothers and sisters in Christ, to pray for us. Pray that in our land, as well, the Word of God might be more widely proclaimed so that many might yet believe in our Lord Jesus Christ. With this, dear friends, I close and extend heartfelt, brotherly greetings. Amen."

We sat in silence for awhile. I had read that some 25,000 Baptists had been imprisoned in the period 1929-45, with a mere 3,000 surviving the ordeal. Between 1945 and 1974 another 20,000 had been imprisoned. Then I thought of the white-haired pastor, sitting right next to me at that morning's service. And I thought of the astounding testimony of Pavel, through whom God had taken the liberating message of the gospel into the inner recesses of the dreaded Siberian prison camps. I remembered that I had among my most treasured possessions the very Bible which tsarist Russian authorities had taken from my grandfather and kept in custody for a year. Yes indeed, ours was a goodly heritage, bought with blood. And so we continued to sit in silence as the late-afternoon sun bathed this wonderful-terrible city in a rosy glow.

8: "Ye Shall Be Witnesses"

More frustrations to plague my intended research program! Despite a year's delay and very specific requests to make use of archival sources, I would not be given access to the archives unless I produced the required documents from central authorities in Moscow. The chief of the archival section in the Library of the Museum of the History of Religion and Atheism, was surprisingly sympathetic.

"I am delighted when anyone comes around to work in the archives, and if it were up to me I would let you in immediately," she insisted, giving every evidence of sincerity. "But, you must understand that I am just a little person. You will need to apply to the central bureau in Moscow."

Already knowing something of the pace of Soviet bureaucratic procedure I realized that such an application would be pointless. We would only be in Leningrad for another two weeks at the most. Was there no alternative?

"Perhaps," she replied rather diffidently, "you could ask our general director. His office is in the former Armenian Church, the blue building just off Nevsky Prospekt."

The office was duly found, though the official in question would not be in for a while. Would I like to wait? This from a rather stern young woman seated behind a plain wooden table in a very spartan reception room. An anticipated few minutes stretched on to half an hour, the secretary relaxing somewhat as we discussed her forth-coming examination in medieval history at the university.

About an hour after I arrived, the director came in, accompanied by a friend. Having identified myself as an exchange fellow interested in the history of the Russian Baptists, I proceeded to the matter of access to the archives. Once again there was the apologetic response: no documents from Moscow; no access to the archives. On the matter of Soviet scholars in my field, he was more helpful. In addition to suggesting some names of younger men who had been working on the subject, he informed me that A. I. Klibanov, who had begun publishing in the 1920s, was still very active. Perhaps I would be able to see him in Moscow.

As I rose to leave, the secretary, who had been listening with great interest, had a question which she was obvi-ously very anxious to ask: "Are you then very rich? Do you have your own airplane?"

I assured her that all I had was a five-year-old car. Wondering what sort of information was being fed to her, I headed back to the Museum library. I would have to make do with the material which I was allowed to use.

As I climbed the stairs up into the dome area of this former cathedral, I remembered a colleague's experience. Soviet scholars had criticized his book for inadequate archival research, but when he had requested access to the appropriate Soviet archives, he had been refused. Instead, his Soviet counterparts suggested that when he had completed his next manuscript he should send it to them. They would then make the necessary corrections in interpretation, based on their reading of the archival material!

The long climb up the circular staircase also gave me opportunity to reflect on the displays below. It seemed that they had left out nothing in their attempt to portray the deception, exploitation, and cruelty that had been carried out in the name of religion. The section on the Spanish Inquisition, with its life-size displays of various tortures, had been especially gruesome. Strangely enough, there was a definite semi-religious quality to the portrayal of the heroic accomplishments of Lenin and the Communist party, struggling to enlighten and liberate the Soviet people and all mankind from the bonds of religious enslavement.

Angry at the terribly distorted picture of both religion and communism, and trying to catch my breath after the long climb, I was not prepared for the smiling clerk who greeted me at the circulation desk with a cheerful, "Welcome back, professor!" Wheezing a bit, I observed that I must be getting older, since the stairs had not bothered me so much the last time. Her quick reply, "Of course you are getting older. The last time you were here was three days ago," helped to improve my disposition. As well, I could derive considerable satisfaction from the fact that I was using atheistically-controlled material to promote a strongly Christian interpretation of the Russian Baptist experience. (We got even greater satisfaction as we used some of the living-expense money, which I received from the Soviet government to help distressed Christians in the USSR.)

The next few hours passed rapidly as I searched through the card catalogues, discovering long-sought materials. After filling in a number of call forms for books to be available the next day, I headed back down the stairs and out into the bright sunshine. It was a welcome contrast to the rather gloomy atmosphere in the museum.

Lil was already waiting for me, engaged in animated conversation with a slim, dark-haired woman in her thirties. An engineer from Siberia, she was in Leningrad on a holiday and happy to meet Westerners, who are rarely seen in the more remote areas of the USSR. Lil had already turned their conversation around to spiritual topics and so it was easy to continue in that vein. Yes, the woman would take the Christian tract which Lil offered her – for her grandmother, who was very interested in these matters and even had an old Bible. Yes, as we suggested, perhaps she would read the material for herself.

That tract had not been the only one which Lil had handed out in the last few days. During a visit to the Hermitage she had stationed herself in front of a medieval painting of Christ. As people stopped to examine the painting she had asked if they knew who the man was. Generally, the persons questioned looked blank and answered negatively. She would then ask if they would like to know, and most replied that they would. They accepted, with thanks, a Russian tract entitled "Who Is Christ?" and moved on, presumably considering Lil to be a museum employee, handing out information pamphlets.

We shared our experiences with Anton and Vera a few days later, much to their delight. Anton agreed that the Museum of the History of Religion and Atheism was an excellent example of both tragedy and farce. It was tragedy, because unsuspecting visitors, bombarded with propaganda about the "scientific" quality of communism, might actually accept the picture of both religion and communism presented there. Yet it was also farce, because of the gross distortions of reality in the presentation of the two belief systems.

"And yet," he continued with an enigmatic smile, "there was a brief period when the gospel was actually being preached there." Intrigued, we pressed him to explain.

"It was when we were living in the downtown area," he began. Vera shuddered involuntarily, interjecting that they had been in a communal apartment, with five families sharing one kitchen and one bathroom. "Well," Anton continued, "I was out for a stroll with our little daughter. As we came up to the museum, for some reason or another I felt compelled to go in. And so we did, joining one of the guided tours which was just beginning.

"You saw the picture of Abraham about to slay Isaac? Well, the guide really got worked up at that point, launching a violent attack on Christianity as a religion of fanaticism, even to the extent of demanding the bloody sacrifice of one's own children. 'Excuse me, Comrade,' I asked, very politely. 'Is it permitted to ask a question?' On being assured that it was, I asked if the picture was an accurate representation of the Biblical record and whether her explanation was also according to the Scriptures. 'Exactly as in the Bible,' she replied vehemently, 'both the picture and my explanation!'

" 'Well,' I answered, 'the picture is accurate, but your explanation is not. God was testing Abraham's faith and obedience. Finding him to be perfectly obedient, God provided a substitute sacrifice in the form of a ram. As you can see in the picture, there is the ram, caught by his horns in a bush.'

"The guide became very flustered and angry, but the people in the tour group were very interested for they had never heard anything like this before. Taking advantage of the guide's temporary silence, I added, 'Of course, the entire incident is a picture of God's sacrifice of His own Son, Jesus Christ. He is, the Lamb, our substitute, bearing the penalty of our sin.'

"Afterwards, a number of our brethren began to drop into the museum on a fairly regular basis. They joined tour groups, asked simple questions and gave Biblical answers. Unfortunately, the museum officials were soon able to spot us and this rather enjoyable ministry was quickly stopped."

"It's certainly not a fair competition," I observed. "The

atheists have access to all the resources of the educational system, the media and cultural centres. The constitution guarantees freedom of anti-religious propaganda only, thus denying freedom of religious propaganda. On a recent trip to the USSR, for example, my mother-in-law was told by a worried relative that she'd better not carry her Bible openly in her hand. That could be considered as conducting religious propaganda. And not content with their monopoly on propaganda – denying the Christians an opportunity to answer charges made against them – the atheists also resort to coercion, using force in an attempt to win an argument."

"Yes," Anton replied, "figuratively speaking, they bind us, gag us, and then beat us with a stick, crying out 'Aha! We have defeated you!' But," he continued, "sometimes the atheists' plans don't work out the way that they expected.

"I occasionally get into discussions with atheist propagandists, either at the plant or in private sessions. One day all of us workers were called into an assembly room to hear one of these agitators. Not surprisingly, along with his attempt to disprove the existence of God, the deity of Christ, miracles and so forth, he attacked me personally. He labelled me 'unprogressive, anti-socialist, and a disruptive influence generally.' When the speaker was finished, the manager, having fulfilled his distasteful task, was about to order us back to work. But the men protested. They know my work record and I believe that they respect me. In the interests of justice, they insisted that since the atheist speaker had attacked both my beliefs and my performance, I should be given an opportunity to state *my* case. The embarrassed manager agreed, and so," Anton chuckled, "I was able to speak to all of them for almost an hour about Christ."

"On another occasion," he continued, warming to his

subject, "one of our brethren somehow managed to get hold of a Moody Institute of Science Film. I was able to borrow a projector and invited a number of people – including one of these atheist propagandists – to see the film in our apartment. As you can see, I had to cut a hole in one wall to get a clearer picture. You know how these atheists pride themselves on being scientific? Well, when the film had ended I asked the atheist what he thought about the accuracy of the science presented. Unable to criticize in any way on scientific grounds, he blustered and sputtered and then snarled; 'One thing I've got to say for you Baptists –you're getting extremely aggressive!' "

"That kind of refusal to face the issues sounds very much like the so-called Yugoslav engineer's response to your question about the orderly universe," Lil observed.

Briefly, I told them about that interesting experience. "Of course," I concluded, "in the light of what had happened during the border crossing and afterwards, I suspect that this engineer had some connections with your own KGB. Incidentally, Anton, have you ever had any personal contact with that organization?"

"He's been interviewed by them so frequently," Vera interjected with a nervous little laugh, "that they call him their 'Minister of External Affairs!' "

"Yes," Anton chuckled, "I've been on numerous visits to their head office here in Leningrad, which we call 'The Big House'. There's a story going around that a visiting American was boasting about the tall buildings in the USA. 'Why,' he said, 'from the Empire State Building, on a clear day, you can see clearly into five states.' Not to be outdone, the Leningrader replied, 'That's nothing! From The Big House, on any kind of day, you can see clearly into Siberia!' "

"That's not really so funny, Anton," said Vera, coming in from the kitchen with a fresh pot of tea. "I keep telling him that his bold witness will get him arrested sooner or later," she continued, filling our cups.

"I do try to speak out for my Lord on every opportunity," he continued, "especially at the plant. It goes without saying that, as a Christian, I do my assigned work as thoroughly and carefully as possible. We must not give the authorities any excuse to label Christians as poor workers and poor citizens. Of course, they do that anyway . . . but my fellow-workers know that they can depend on me. As we all know, there's more than enough shoddy work because of poor planning, lack of incentive, and drunkenness. We've had trucks sitting idle for three weeks because of delay in getting a single part from a factory right here in Leningrad.

"In that apartment block next to us you can pretty well tell which parts were constructed in the morning, when the workers were sober, and which in the afternoon, when they were not. For that matter, nothing was being done on that construction project until just before it was supposed to be completed. Then they worked around the clock, finishing on time – except for one thing. They had forgotten to put in the plumbing and the connections with the sewer. For several days the place was a madhouse. Jackhammers were going day and night as they smashed through pavement and concrete walls to be able to put in the necessary pipes.

"I remember when I was servicing new cars. They would arrive from the factory with all the gauges, handles, windshield wipers and other removable parts missing. We would be three weeks getting this new car repaired and ready for the owner. You may know that it takes about five years wages, paid in advance, to get the cheapest car here – and that there is a five-year waiting period?

"But I have been wandering," Anton laughed. "It's just that so many workers are totally different from the efficient, diligent, public-spirited 'typical Soviet workers' portrayed in official propaganda. In actual fact, oddly enough, it is the Christians who are the ideal Soviet workers.

"Anyway," he continued, "perhaps it is partly because of my work record that the men are willing to listen to me when I talk to them of Christ. The manager had threatened to fire me if I did not stop and one day he ordered me to go to his office. A KGB officer was waiting to question me about my activities. I answered his questions about my work simply and straightforwardly, after which I began to speak to him of his own need of salvation.

"Up to this time our conversation had been quite businesslike, but now he became very angry. 'Don't you know who I am?' he fairly shouted, 'I have the power, with a word, to send you to Siberia!'

" 'I know that you are a man,' I replied, 'and that you have an undying soul. On the other hand, if you were a cow, I would not have to speak to you about spiritual matters!' And so our conversation continued, the Lord enabling me to present the claims of Christ to this hardened police officer. After about an hour of this we shook hands and he left. I went back to my work area, not knowing what to expect.

"An hour later I was called into the manager's office again. 'I can't understand it!' said the manager in a quieter voice than he had ever used in speaking to me before. 'The KGB officer informed me that I must in no way consider firing you – that you are the best worker in the entire plant. And after you called him a cow!' "

Chuckling at the memory of the incident, Anton held out his cup for a refill. " 'No, I did not call him a cow', I answered. 'I merely said that if he were a cow I would not have to talk to him about his soul.' And you know," he concluded, settling back into his chair and grinning

[73]

delightedly, "while explaining the whole situation to the manager I felt compelled to describe the way of salvation to him as well."

On our way to the evening service at the Polkonaia Gora church, Anton continued his recollections of some of the opportunities he'd had recently to bear witness. "It was just about here," he said as we came up to a traffic light, "that a police officer stopped me one day. I guess I must have been thinking about something or other and failed to notice that the light had changed. Anyway, when the officer asked for my documents, I included a Gospel of John. He was going to hand it back when he had finished examining the documents, but I told him to keep it. 'What am I supposed to do with it – pray to it?' he sneered. 'No,' I replied, 'it's a very good little book; just read it.'

"About a week later, I was driving along this same road again and, remembering the light, I was being especially careful. Suddenly, there was that same officer, signalling me to pull over. I wondered what I had done wrong this time. But he came over to the car, stuck his head through the open window, and asked, 'Do you have any more books like that? I really enjoyed reading it!' "

"Well," I laughed, "it is clear that you are one of those who, like the apostles, cannot help but speak of the things that you have seen and heard. But is this sort of witnessing common to believers in general in the USSR? Quite apart from official prohibition of religious propaganda, there must be considerable family and social pressure against witnessing. Surely, unbelieving family members would not want to risk their jobs, apartments, or children's career opportunities because of the active witness of a Christian relative? This is what my mother-in-law discovered in our home village in the Ukraine. And unbelievers in general, trying to gain favour and possible privileges from the authorities, would certainly be hostile to vigorous, visible witnessing. It seems to me," I continued, "that I have read somewhere recently in a Western publication that Soviet Christians have been reduced to silence."

"Of course," Anton replied, "there is a price to be paid for active witnessing, and a number of our brethren have experienced the kinds of losses which you have mentioned. In my experience, however, both the social and political situations have much in common. In both cases, it is the zealots who apply pressure, while the indifferent or lazy leave us alone. Overall," he continued, turning around to make his point face-to-face (and leaving the car to drive itself) "despite what you have heard at home, let me assure you that except for a small minority, all believers in the USSR are witnessing all the time, everywhere!"

He whirled around in response to Vera's scream, narrowly missing an oncoming truck. "Yes," he continued, apparently unruffled, "all of us are witnessing. Isn't that the way it is in the West as well?"

"Our situation would seem to be the reverse of yours," I replied. "We have the freedom; you do not. Your cost is the prospect of serious losses; ours is, at the most, some personal embarrassment or social non-acceptance. Here, only a minority is *not* witnessing; there, only a minority *is* witnessing."

We had arrived at the church, and I looked around eagerly to find the new friend whom we had met at the birthday party. Would he have remembered to bring the promised booklet? In a few minutes I spotted him standing alone for the moment at the corner of an outbuilding. Moving quickly up to him I gave him the traditional embrace and asked quietly if he had the booklet with him, as arranged.

"Yes," he replied, "but I can't give it to you out here in the yard, with all those people watching. Let's go downstairs in the church."

This suited me perfectly, since I wanted to see Pastor Fadukhin on another matter. As we walked down the steps, my friend slipped the booklet out of an inner pocket and I transferred it to a similarly safe place.

I had arranged to meet Fadukhin for an interview on Wednesday and wanted to check if that was still satisfactory. He was seated with a number of other preaching brethren in the church office and greeted me graciously. "Well, brother," he asked, "how is your research going?"

"Pretty well," I replied, "despite some difficulties with the bureaucrats. But I had an interesting experience at the Academy of Sciences library the other day, thanks to my wife. We had spent a pleasant day out at the Summer Palace, enjoying the rapid hydrofoil ride and thrilled by the magnificent fountains. An unexpected 'plus' was a very good supper at the Hotel Astoria. As you know, this is where Hitler had planned his victory banquet – which was never held, thanks to the heroism of Leningrad's defenders. I was all set to stay in our hotel room, but my wife kept insisting that I should put in a few hours' work at the library.

"Somewhat reluctantly I agreed to go, finding that a number of the old journals which I had ordered were waiting for me. As I arranged them on my desk a distinguished looking man of about seventy came up to me.

"Pointing at one of the journals he asked, '*Slovo istiny (The Word of Truth)* – what kind of a journal is that?' I answered that this was a Baptist journal, reminding him of Christ's claim to be the Truth. I also mentioned that there was a Baptist church right here in Leningrad on Poklonaia Gora. He asked if he might read the journal and then proceeded to read sermons for an hour and a half. When he returned the journal he thanked me. Curious, I asked him of his profession, to which he replied that he was a retired physics professor from the Academy of Sciences. The reluctant evening trip to the library had been very much worthwhile," I concluded.

"Yes," said Fadukhin, "we too have had some of those from higher positions come to visit us sometimes, like Nicodemus, by night. Recently, for example, an editor of one of the top publications in Leningrad came to visit me. He informed me that he was tired of spreading lies and had heard that the truth was to be found among us. A similar incident involved a professor from the university. God is beginning to speak to people from all walks of life in our country.

"But I'm afraid I have some bad news for you," he sighed. "I have an important executive meeting which has suddenly come up and thus I'll not be able to meet with you on Wednesday morning. And," he added, with a mixture of regret and relief, "since you are leaving for Moscow in a few days, we'll not be able to meet at a later date. My suggestion that we could meet when I came back to Leningrad early in July was met by a polite, but unenthusiastic, "It will be good to see you again."

I mentioned this to Anton on the way back to our hotel after the service. "Perhaps some 'higher up' has suggested to Fadukhin that he should not meet with me," I commented. "Maybe this was another example of cooperative Baptist Union officials in Moscow receiving orders from the government and then pressuring the local church to fall into line? As a matter of fact," I concluded, "was it not this problem of central Union officials meddling in local church matters that split the Baptist movement into Union and Reform segments in the 1960s?"

"There has been a lot of official pressure lately against undue contacts with foreigners," Anton replied, "and it is possible that Fadukhin was warned. That may indeed be one of the reasons why you have not been asked to speak at the services. As for meddling in local church affairs, it has been our experience that the Reform leadership has actually done more of that than the old Union leadership does. Brother Stepan, pastor of the Independent church at . . ., for example, used to be part of the Reform Council of Churches. But now that he has registered his church as independent of either union, the Reformers are calling him a schismatic."

Anton's view of central-local relations and general conditions within the Union and Reform associations was rather different from the picture presented in some poorly-informed Western Christian publications. According to those publications, labels are very simple and are very easily attached. All Union churches are described as registered, sold out to the government, and under the thumb of Union officials in Moscow, who are nothing but Kremlin stooges. Contrarily, all Reform churches are described as unregistered, forced to meet underground, maintain a heroic independence of government control, and are thoroughly self-governing, though freely joined together in an ultra-democratic Reform association.

Reality is much more complicated. With respect to their relationships to one another, Baptist churches can be classified as belonging to the old Union (1944), the Reformers' Council of Churches (1965) or Independent. In each of the three categories an individual church might be either registered or unregistered. Thus, Anton told us of at least ten churches, including a very large one in Tashkent in Central Asia and several in the Ukraine, which were Independent, and registered as such.

"Is the situation in Leningrad typical of that in the USSR generally?" I asked, as we pulled into a deserted side street near our hotel.

"Officially", he answered, "the two unions have no fellowship with one another. The Council of Churches has taken the position that true fellowship will not be possible until the old Union repents for its close collaboration with state officials. Relationships between the two Baptist groups at the local level can vary widely. In some cases the local situation is just as tense as the central one, while in others, some attempts at reconciliation are taking place. In Leningrad we have all three kinds of churches: the Union one on Poklonaia Gora; a Council of Churches group with about 170 members in the suburb of Kuzmolovo; and our own Independent, unregistered assembly of about 70 members at Gorelovo.

"I was present at two conferences called to discuss the special problems of believers in our land and to decide how churches having different views should relate to one another. Overall, we have decided to maintain peaceful relations and keep up contacts with all our brethren. In our Gorelovo church we see the independent local church as the pillar and ground of the truth. And though we want to live peacefully with all our brethren, apart from bringing in some of these brethren as we see the need of their advice and counsel, we insist that all questions be settled internally, strictly by our own membership.

"In pursuit of contacts and fellowship, we extended an invitation to the brethren at the Poklonaia Gora church to participate in our harvest festival services last year. They responded warmly and we celebrated joyfully together, with men from both churches preaching, both choirs singing, and so forth. In turn, they invited us to share in their harvest festival where our presbyter, another preaching brother and I were called on to preach.

"After that service we had a brief discussion with the leaders at the Poklonaia Gora church concerning our future relationship, indicating our desire to be at peace with them. We added that while we have our differences on internal matters, this should not separate us – we are brethren! They joyfully accepted our suggestions and told us that we should feel free to come to their services and preach, not only on special occasions, but at any time.

"And so it was," he concluded, "in the providence of God, that we met you and have had this wonderful fellowship."

It was very hard to say good-bye. Our two-week acquaintance, so full of laughter and tears, had created depths of friendship and sharing that might have taken years in another context. A last warm embrace and brotherly kiss and we watched the heroic little Zaporozhets bouncing cheerfully along the cobblestoned street. Anton's sturdy arm flailed a final good-bye as they turned a corner.

We walked into the lobby of the familiar Oktiabrskaia Hotel, picking up our key from the pleasant blonde desk clerk who had frequently loaned us her electric kettle for morning coffee. What was waiting for us at Moscow?

9: *Expect the Unexpected*

Our already full suitcases protested against the books, children's gifts, and silver tea-glass holders which we tried to cram into them. But finally everything was packed and the suitcases were ready to be locked. The smaller one presented no problem, but the little padlock for the larger one seemed to have disappeared. Painstaking search failed to discover it; so, I decided to run the six blocks to the hardware store to buy another little padlock.

I returned out of breath, beginning to feel a little anxious about getting to the station on time. Frustration mounted when I discovered that the hasp on the bulky padlock – the only one available in the store – would not go through the holes on the suitcase zipper pulls.

"I guess we'll just have to travel with an unlocked suitcase," I fumed. "Why did this all have to happen today, of all days?" I complained to no one in particular as I left to settle our hotel bill.

By this time our friendly blonde desk clerk had been replaced by a grim-looking stranger. According to her calculations I owed them approximately thirty rubles more than I had been expecting to pay. I knew of the five ruble per day charge for the extra person in the room, but what unknown services or facilities were represented by this additional thirty rubles?

She looked at me uncomprehendingly. "But it's right there on the bill," she explained. "It is for the television set and the refrigerator which all visiting scholars request."

"This visiting scholar certainly did not request a television set," I retorted, "and there is no refrigerator in the room."

"But of course there is a refrigerator in the room," she insisted. "The television set is sitting right on top of it."

"You mean that white, box-like thing?" I asked. "But we assumed that it was simply the television stand. Had we known it was a refrigerator we might have had an easier time with our time-consuming shopping. At any rate," I concluded, "I did not ask for the refrigerator or the television, and I don't see why I should be charged for them!"

"I'm sorry," she replied – quite warmly – "but I have my orders. If you wish, you can take it up with the manager."

Not waiting for the unreliable elevator I tore down the stairs and found the manager's office. Rather vehemently, I stated my case. He listened stonily and insisted that the full amount must be paid. As I strode angrily toward the door he suggested calmly that he could try to bill the University of Leningrad for the extra amount.

"No," I replied curtly, "I'll pay it myself. And I'll have a nice souvenir of my experiences on the academic exchange program."

The manager had obviously called the desk clerk. She was all smiles and sympathetic cooings. "No," she insisted, "you must not pay the additional thirty rubles. The charges for the refrigerator and the television will be assumed by the university. Everything has been settled. Have a pleasant trip to Moscow," she called out graciously as I marched down the corridor.

"Look at the time," I groaned as I got back to our room. Some additional items had been discovered, making it necessary to re-pack our already impossibly full suitcases. Frustration, anger, and the steady ticking of the clock did nothing to improve my packing efficiency. "Why?", I sputtered, "Why, why, why?"

"Maybe," Lil said softly, "it is God's way of teaching you to be more sympathetic with the people who have to put up with the Soviet system every day. And maybe," she added very gently, "you needed to learn to master some rather un-Christian irritability."

It was a chastened, but much more cheerful man who hoisted the bulging suitcases on to the Moscow-bound train. Clearly, in addition to providing an opportunity to discover my spiritual roots, this visit to the USSR could teach me all sorts of valuable lessons.

"We don't often see Western tourists on our trains," said a short, dark-haired man about thirty years of age. "Where are you from – America?"

I identified myself and introduced Lil. He shook her hand graciously and gestured toward the slim, attractive young woman settling into a seat just down the aisle.

"And that is my wife, Tanya," he said. "We're on our way to a three-week holiday in the Caucasus. Are you going to visit the South as well on this trip?"

"Well," I replied, "we *are* going to Kiev."

"But that is not *really* the South," he laughed, "– at least, not compared with the Caucasus or the southernmost parts of Central Asia. Any way, if you don't mind my asking, what is your field of interest?"

"I'm writing a history of the Russian Baptists in the pre-Revolutionary period," I answered, adding that my interests were both academic and personal since both Lil and I shared the Russian Baptists' convictions.

"Well," he replied, "both my wife and I are Jewish. But with us it's not so much a religious as a cultural thing. Of course," he added, "I am well-acquainted with the teachings of Judaism and I have even done a certain amount of reading about other religions. I know, for example, that the Baptists are Protestants, but what are their distinctive beliefs?"

He stood there in the aisle, nodding as I mentioned belief in the Scriptures as the divinely-inspired, infallible Word of God and the sole authority in matters of faith and practice. Other beliefs such as justification by faith, the believers' church and believers' baptism by immersion required some explanation, as did the specific nature of Baptist views on freedom of conscience and the separation of church and state. We were delighted to have this unexpected opportunity to share our faith. We were also pleasantly surprised when one or the other of us managed to find the right Russian words to explain various concepts to our very patient listener.

And so the conversation went on, ranging over such topics as the independent reality of spiritual life, the positive contributions of Christianity, and the crucial importance of a personal relationship with God through faith in Jesus Christ. Though his observations tended to be sharply critical, they were always offered in an objective and not unpleasant manner. He willingly accepted a Russian-language leaflet listing various topics and giving appropriate Biblical references.

Wishing us a pleasant stay in his country he straightened up and stretched to relieve the strain from an hour-long bending over the back of a seat during our conversation. Eyes moving rapidly over the leaflet, he headed back to where his wife was dozing. Here was another one of those 'accidental' meetings which we would experience in the USSR. It was similar to the one which Lil had had with the two American women in Leningrad, suppliers of the leaflet given to our Jewish travelling companion. The Moscow portion of our trip, now that we had actually begun it, was off to a promising start.

"I'm sure he'll be hearing the gospel again soon," Lil

commented as we settled back into our seats. "After all, he told us that he lives in Leningrad, and we've already seen how aggressively those Christians witness."

"That's true," I replied. "Maybe Anton will meet him some time – or even give him the tape we left with him in Leningrad – you know, the one the Americans said had been specially prepared to present Christ to Soviet Jews?"

As the express train rattled along, taking us ever further from Leningrad, our minds, as if to compensate, kept returning to that now familiar city. It had been the perfect starting point for our visit, a city at once Western and Russian, old and new. Three weeks of almost daily sightseeing had been insufficient to tap the riches of old St. Petersburg, Russia's social and cultural, as well as political capital for two hundred years. Apart from the failure to gain access to archival sources my research had been very profitable. Materials which I had searched for throughout America and Europe for ten years had been discovered in Leningrad's libraries. A list of one hundred items had been left with the International Department of the Saltykov-Shchedrin Library for duplication.

We had walked almost everywhere, criss-crossing the compact central core of this city of four million. It was a magnificent city, its planned symmetry balanced by the rainbow range of its stuccoed buildings, its overall horizontalness by the gold and green spires and domes of its old churches. Imposing buildings, broad avenues, heroic-sized squares, statues and monuments gave us an overwhelming impression of the might and majesty of the Russian/Soviet state.

But there was also the more intimate Leningrad of narrow cobble-stoned side streets, alive with noisy boys playing soccer and giggling girls, skipping, cuddling favorite dolls, sharing secrets. Shuffling laborers and sophisticated white-collar workers, weary mothers with food-filled string bags and smartly-dressed secretaries alert for any rumor of scarce and stylish imports – none was too busy to tell us about their beautiful city. Patient old men smiled indulgently at their impatient, chattering grandsons as they sat together on stone railings, their long fishing poles extended hopefully over the Neva's grey waters. Baby-sitting grandmothers gossiped on park benches while their little darlings frolicked on the grass or slept peacefully in expensive baby carriages.

For most visitors Leningrad was Imperial Russia's capital and cultural center, cradle of the Revolution and Hero-City of World War II. We would remember it primarily for the impact of its Christians. A hostile political and social environment raises the price of Christian commitment to very high levels. But persecution also makes for purity, with the attendant beauty of character and spiritual power that strengthens fellow-believers and attracts outsiders. Having so little, they risked losing all by their aggressive witnessing. Though menaced, maligned and materially poor, they seemed to be suffused with an unquenchable joy, and their prayers were filled with praise to God for His blessings to them.

They had inspired us. They had also, in the words of a comfortable Canadian believer, "made us thoroughly ashamed of our own Christianity." What was the little we had given them in money or literature in comparison with the massive object lesson they had given us? Our supposedly deep theological and doctrinal comments had been received with humble respect by those whose daily lives reflected, naturally and spontaneously, the very heart of Christianity.

Most devastating of all, those who prayed with the power of an Abraham, Elijah or Paul had asked us to pray for them. Oh yes, they would appreciate whatever literature we could get to them. And it might help if we publicized their needs and petitioned their government to give them greater practical religious liberty. But everywhere we went, among Christians from every walk of life, the request was always the same: "Pray for us!"

When asked what we should pray for specifically their answers were also always the same. One heard echoes of the traditional Russian search for wholeness, along with the reflection of an obvious need for Christian solidarity in an atheist land. Above all, there was the longing to actualize Christ's prayer "that they all may be one". Everywhere and always it was the same fervent plea: "Pray with us that there might be unity among the brethren!"

The conductor's voice broke into our reminiscing. "We will arrive at the station in ten minutes." Pleasant recollections of Leningrad gave way to apprehensions about Moscow. According to friends who had visited both cities, their respective atmospheres were very different. According to them, Moscow seemed more medieval-Russian, bureaucratically rigid, impersonal. We were entering the very heart of the Soviet Union, the seat of its dictatorial government, implacable enemy of the West and its values. This was the command center of atheism's half-century war against religion in general and our fellow-Baptists in particular. Moscow was also the headquarters of the All-Union Council of Evangelical Christians-Baptists, the old Union governing body, with its reputation for bowing the knee before atheist officialdom. The five thousand-member Moscow Baptist church was something of a showplace, much given to entertaining visiting dignitaries of all faiths. What sort of reception would we receive there?

The train had stopped. Tired and grubby after our ten-hour trip, we were looking forward to a hot shower and a comfortable bed at the University Hotel. But given the efficiency of the Soviet bureaucracy that might be a long way off.

"I hope Leningrad University remembered to make the reservation," I muttered to Lil as we wriggled through the crowds.

The taxi driver grunted as he hoisted our over-stuffed luggage into the trunk. Informing him that we wanted to go to the University Hotel we settled down into the back seat of the surprisingly comfortable cab. He drove off muttering to himself.

"University Hotel, University Hotel? I wonder where that could be?"

A few blocks from the station he hailed a fellow-cabbie across the street. "Hey friend, you wouldn't happen to know where the University Hotel is?"

"Yeah," came the slightly sarcastic answer, "it's over by the university. It's right beside the shop called *Balaton*. You've never been there before?"

As we drove rapidly down the brightly-lit, four-lane road we had the sensation of being in a large Canadian city. Reflections of street lamps and office building lights sparkled on the river waters as we crossed the bridge, dozens of cars whizzing by us in both directions. Lil and I looked at one another and smiled. Perhaps, after all, it was not Leningrad but *Moscow* that would prove to be 'a real city'.

"Well, here we are," the driver announced cheerily. "Two rubles fifty, please." Though tipping is officially non-existent, my suggestion that he keep the change from a three-ruble bill brought no protest. He helped us carry our luggage into the crowded hotel lobby and waved a friendly good-bye.

There were long lines in front of the reservation wickets, but a pleasant-looking young clerk stood all by herself at an adjacent counter, checking some papers.

1 The evangelical church in Borodianka, Kiev province. The author's grandfather, the Rev. Nestor A Nesdoly, was one of the pioneers of this church.

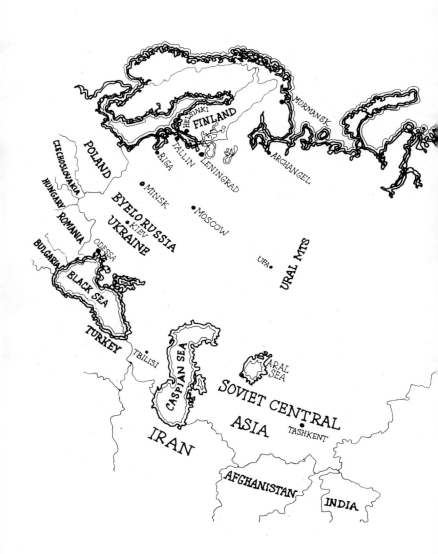

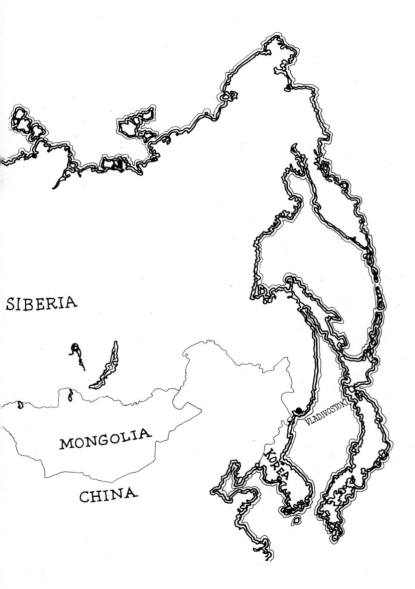

SIBERIA

MONGOLIA

CHINA

VLADIVOSTOK

KOREA

2 A map of the USSR showing places referred to in the book.

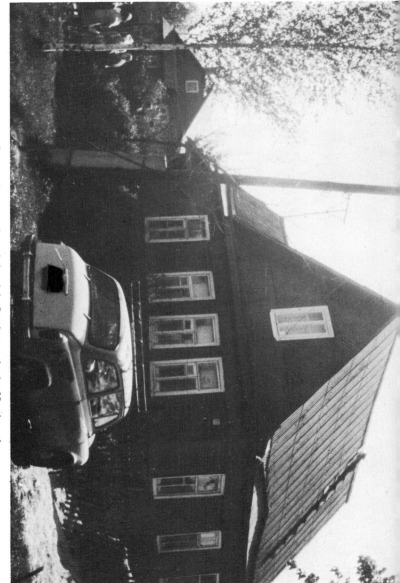

3 Independent unregistered church in Gorelovo, suburb of Leningrad.

4 Darnetskaia church, Kiev, a registered, Union congregation (Pastor Vladimir Kunets).

5 Map of USSR, Hermitage Museum, Leningrad

6 The strength of the Soviet evangelicals – prayer. The wall sign reads 'God is love'.

7 The author and his wife.

8 Poklonaia Gora church (a registered, Union congregation), Leningrad.

"Professor and Mrs. Nesdoly, from Canada? Yes, we've been expecting you. You must be tired after that long train ride. Register?" she asked incredulously, in response to my question. "You are already registered. Vanya, come here and take these bags up to room 405," she called to a lanky young man. "Have a good night's rest," she said cheerily as we headed towards the elevator.

I looked at my watch. We had been in the hotel for approximately five minutes. Truly, as Peter the Great had observed, "Russia is a country in which that which cannot happen, happens." I even found our original little padlock as soon as I opened the smaller suitcase that evening.

10: *East is East and West is West?*

It was already after nine when we awoke and there was mail waiting for us at the Canadian Embassy on Staraia Koniushnaia Ulitsa (literally, Old Stable Street). The clerks in the souvenir shop were very helpful, suggesting that we take the tram for 3 kopeks (5¢Cdn.) to the nearest subway station. In a few minutes we were rattling along past Moscow State University, its massive main building done in the wedding-cake style popular in Stalin's era. On arrival at the subway station we noticed a long queue. An enterprising Muscovite was selling California lemons to eager buyers.

We were impressed with the cleanliness and efficiency of the subway system, wondering if any other city could boast a uniform eight-cent (5 kopek) fare, regardless of distance travelled. Each station was decorated differently; all were attractive; some were absolutely magnificent with their marble or brass pillars and huge crystal chandeliers. Checking our map as we rode we familiarized ourselves with the routes which we expected to take. In a few minutes we had arrived at our stop. After a *long* escalator ride we emerged into a busy, tree-lined street. Not too far away was one of the world's largest swimming pools. Even if that Muscovite boast might be contested, this was surely the largest outdoor pool used on a year-round basis – despite Moscow's prolonged, frigid winters.

An official-looking man of about fifty gave us quick directions to the Canadian Embassy, and the militia officer at the entrance waved us in after scrutinizing our passports. The maple-leaf flag, familiar portraits, magazines and papers, the eagerly-awaited mail, gave us the sense of being back home.

We stood for a moment with an embassy employee, admiring the comfortable lounge. "Well," I laughed, "at least this is one place in the USSR where we can speak freely." The young man shook his head slowly and looked meaningfully toward the ceiling, making upward-jabbing motions with an extended index finger.

I wondered if he was being overly suspicious, remembering the experience of one of the players on a visiting Canadian hockey team. The hockey player had noticed a suspicious-looking bump in the carpet in his hotel room. Closer investigation revealed it to be a perforated dome-shaped object – obviously some sort of listening device! Thinking to take it home as a souvenir of his trip to the USSR, he began to undo the nuts on the three bolts by which this listening device was attached to the subfloor. The first two were fairly easy, the last one considerably more difficult, but it too finally yielded. There was a sudden resounding crash. Subsequent investigation revealed that the alleged listening device was actually holding up the chandelier in the room below.

We mentioned this to Marion, a vivacious Ontario redhead who worked in the embassy. "When I first got here," she laughed, "it seemed as if the KGB was deliberately trying to put me on edge. I'd come home to my apartment one day to find an earring missing from the dresser-top; the next day the missing earring would reappear. Once I came home at noon to get something I'd forgotten, only to find the kettle still hot and my instant coffee jar in a different place. But then I found that I could use the system.

"I had gone down to the special diplomatic grocery store where I do most of my food shopping. It's not as good as the supermarkets back home, but it's a lot better-stocked than any of the regular grocery stores here in Moscow. Anyway, I got this craving for bananas, but there were none at the store. I came back to my apartment and said – very loudly – to relieve my feelings: 'This is some backward country! You can't even get bananas in the capital city!' Later that afternoon I went back to the store and saw the same clerk who had served me that morning. Pointing to the freshly-filled bin I said – ever so politely, of course – 'I'll have a kilo of those lovely bananas, please!' "

I left to look after the details of my research at the Lenin Library and Lil went off to do some sightseeing. We agreed to meet with Marion and a friend from Canada back at the embassy later in the afternoon. After a quick "Marion-special" tour of one section of Moscow we would go to a Bible study at the home of the American embassy's military attaché.

The library was impressive, housing over thirty million volumes – yet another Soviet candidate for largest in the world. In Room Number One, reserved for senior scholars, both Soviet and foreign, the atmosphere was suitably refined and the clerks very respectful. Requested catalogues appeared quickly, and I was delighted to discover several long-sought works that had not been available in Leningrad. Wanting to make the best use of my time I decided simply to list things for microfilming, rather than reading and taking copious notes. My status as an academic exchange fellow entitled me to special treatment: up to 2,000 pages of microfilming per day, and at a very low cost.

The lines had fallen unto us in pleasant places. We had a comfortable hotel room for which there would be no extra charge. The transportation system was superb. The mail from our children had arrived, along with some letters from

Christian friends in Canada. In case of any emergency we had easy access to the embassy, one of whose officials was already making arrangements for me to interview a Soviet scholar. I had discovered some prize sources and was receiving VIP treatment in one of the world's largest libraries. Tonight we would be meeting Christians from several countries for an international Bible study. All of this had happened within twenty-four hours of our arrival in Moscow. Praise God from whom all blessings flow!

Lil reported that she had had a good day as well, touring Tolstoy's Moscow home, a wooden building in an old part of the city. She had been wondering if some of these buildings had survived the great fire of 1812, during the Napoleonic occupation. When she asked some elderly women about this they all looked blank. Finally a cheerful octogenarian responded.

"Well, little daughter," she wheezed sympathetically, "I don't know what they tell you tourists. But I can assure you that there has never been any fire here. I should know," she continued proudly. "After all, I've been living in Moscow for fifty years!"

We were still sharing the day's experiences when Marion drove up. She introduced us to Jim, a lanky twenty-year-old from Hamilton, Ontario. He reminded us of our own son, partly because of his irrepressible wit and partly because of his six-foot-five height. He folded himself into the front seat of the car after Lil and I had jammed ourselves into the back.

"Well," I sighed, "here at last we four Canadians in the USSR can speak freely about anything at all."

Marion shook her head, gesturing meaningfully. "As soon as an embassy employee buys a car, Soviet authorities insist that skilled Soviet mechanics 'service' it, making sure that it is safe to drive," she explained.

Apart from the drive along the riverbank and through that section of Moscow in which the government leaders have estate-like homes, the tour was not especially interesting. There were the now-familiar clusters of apartment blocks, already shabby-looking though but recently constructed. But the workers who lived in these apartments at least had the advantage of being in the capital city. Fellow-workers in provincial cities might not see meat in their stores for four months at a stretch. A bitter riddle asks, "Is it possible for a man to ride a horse three days from Leningrad to Moscow?" The answer is "No, because meat-starved people would have eaten the horse by the time the rider reached Novgorod." And far from sympathizing with their less-fortunate fellow-citizens, Muscovites resented the frequent shopping raids of these deprived outsiders.

"You'll want to visit one of Moscow's produce markets," Marion suggested, gesturing toward a large building. "The prices are a lot higher than in the state stores, but the quality is a lot better. And you'll enjoy talking to the farmers – they're amazingly friendly."

"It's only since coming to the USSR that I've really begun to appreciate the free enterprise system," Lil laughed.

"The collective farmers selling on the open market obviously appreciate it too," I added. "It says something about the Soviet economy, doesn't it? Private plots make up about two per cent of the cultivated area, but they provide some forty per cent of the fresh produce."

"The Georgians are the real wheeler-dealers," Marion chuckled. "You should see them coming from the airport with their huge suitcases full of exorbitantly-priced grapes and other fruit. And the people buy them out in minutes."

"Ironic, isn't it," I observed, "that backward Imperial Russia was a grain exporter and a country of over-flowing farmers' markets, but that advanced Soviet Russia imports grain and experiences constant shortages. Of course, life has improved in many ways since 1917 in terms of state-supported education, medical and social services and cultural opportunities. But thanks to the régime's military and heavy industry bias and the privileges granted to various élites, ordinary citizens just don't get the kind of consumer goods and services available to their counterparts in Europe or North America."

Mercifully, Marion broke into this excerpt from one of my university lectures. "We embassy employees feel so sorry for the Russians who do cleaning or maintenance for us. In response to their pleas and to show our appreciation for their work, we sometimes buy things for them in the foreign currency shops. But lately," she sighed, "our supervisors have told us to stop, warning us not to get too attached to any Soviet citizens. Unscrupulous police officials could use that friendship to try to force us into giving them information, by threatening to harm our Russian friends."

After a couple of wrong turns we arrived at an apartment complex housing members of the diplomatic community. "Pay no attention to that glowering militia officer," Marion advised as we made our way into an inner courtyard.

The buildings were not very different from those seen on our afternoon drive, and the elevator only slightly less dingy than the one we remembered so well from our visits with Anton and Vera in Leningrad. But the Robertson's apartment was unlike anything we had seen in the USSR. Spacious, thickly-carpeted, elegantly-furnished, its large, ultra-modern kitchen equipped with the latest-model appliances – it was a comfortable middle-class American island in the Soviet sea. Presumably, élite members of the Soviet Union's classless society enjoyed comparable accommodation.

The Bible study was delightful, led by a gracious Chinese gentleman whose wife was an officer in the Singaporean Embassy. Representatives of the United Kingdom, New Zealand, the US and Canada rounded out the international Christian community. Given the likelihood of hidden listening devices, we were advised to be general in our comments and in our prayers, but to speak out as loudly and clearly as we could.

On hearing that I was involved in research on the Russian Baptists, the chaplain asked if I could fill him in on contemporary conditions. Delighted with this opportunity to talk on a favorite subject I was about to begin when he suggested meaningfully that we should go for a stroll. There was a gas station nearby and his car was very low on fuel. We could talk for the twenty minutes it would take to walk there and back.

"I'd drive down," he explained, "but I'm not sure we would make it – or if my car has been 'serviced,' if you know what I mean."

We returned in time to share in the coffee and thickly-iced chocolate layer cake. Animated conversation continued for another two hours as Anglicans, Baptists, Brethren, Pentecostals and Presbyterians from the four corners of the earth found that in Christ there is no East or West. We left reluctantly, eagerly accepting an invitation to continue the visit a week later over a Chinese supper with our new friends from Singapore.

11: *"You Never Know Whom You Will Meet in Church"*

By Sunday we were using the subway system with ease and had found the most direct route to the Baptist church on Malo-Vuzovskii Pereulok. Now, rocking along in the tram, we looked around at the other passengers. Our attention was drawn to two men in their sixties, one portly, the other rather gaunt. They got off at our stop and headed in the direction of the church. We exchanged introductions and greetings, laughing as we discovered that they had been thinking the same thing we had: "Those two people over there must be Christians."

The stout one was a preacher from the Moscow area. His companion, a retired office worker from the Crimea, was a descendant of those Dukhobors who had returned to Russia after migrating to Canada. He and many of his co-religionists had experienced conversion in the homeland and had joined Baptist congregations. Had the same kind of thing happened among Canadian Dukhobors?

"Only to a very limited extent," Lil answered, mentioning that there were numerous Dukhobors on her father's side of the family. Further conversation indicated that our new acquaintance was probably even a distant relative.

Within minutes this "family connection" had been extended to include some of his relatives. "You must meet my niece," he said enthusiastically. "After all, she's also a sort of relative of your's. She a pharmacist by profession, one of five daughters of a Baptist pastor in the Urals. I'll take you out for lunch and introduce you to her at the afternoon service."

The man in charge of greeting visitors that morning was helpful, showing us into a library/office containing books, journals, pictures and records relating to Russian Baptist history. In addition to this central church with its 5,000 members, he informed us, there were fourteen other churches, each having from 300–350 members, in sub-urban Moscow.

As Lil and I moved toward the visitors' section in the balcony we noticed a display of colorful leaflets on a large table. Most of them were in the English language and all of them praised the Soviet government's accomplishments in economic and social development, general human progress, and especially peace promotion. Given traditional Baptist views on church-state separation, this open political propaganda was unusual, to say the least. It was also unusual to see a Baptist church welcoming a delegation of Mormon students from Brigham Young University. But then this *was* the Moscow Baptist Church.

We settled into the front-row bench in the balcony as the morning service began. As expected, some visiting American Baptists brought greetings, though the anticipated Mormon choir participation did not occur. The church choir, accompanied by a pipe organ and several stringed instruments, was magnificent. Its featured soprano soloist was probably good enough to sing with one of the state opera companies. The sermons were indistinguishable from those we had heard in the Union and Independent churches in Leningrad. Especially touching was the simple message by an eighty-four-year-old saint. He reminded us that, for the Christian, fear of God involved the fear born of love: fear lest we should grieve our loving Heavenly Father.

After the service the Mormon visitors passed through the congregation, smiling and shaking hands with the adults, distributing gum and candy to the children and young people. Each gift came wrapped in a piece of Mormon literature.

"Greetings, friends! So good to see you again," said Sergei, coming up to us. He was one of the young preaching brethren whom we had met at the Poklonaia Gora church in Leningrad. Graduate of Spurgeon's College, speaking excellent English and widely travelled in the West, Sergei had a great future in the Baptist Union. He would shortly be named a senior presbyter.

"Do you happen to know who those fellows are?" I asked, pointing to a couple of smartly-dressed young men distributing their gifts to a group of children.

"Some Americans, by the look of them," he replied casually. "They're always visiting here."

"They're Mormons," Lil and I chorused. "and they're distributing their literature."

"Mormons!" he almost shrieked. Spotting Pastor Mikhail Zhidkov getting ready to drive off, he rushed toward the car shouting, "Misha, Misha! Wait a minute; there's something very important I have to tell you!"

Our new-found relative appeared and we began to walk the few blocks to the dining room which he had chosen. It was not one which we would have chosen, even though it was nearby and very economical. We picked up our unappetizing food cafeteria-style. Grim-faced men wearing spattered aprons and armed with large ladles stood behind the greasy serving counter. Any delay in choosing between various kinds of anonymous-looking "stews" brought fourth an impatient snarl: "Well, well what do you want? Others are waiting to be served." In desperation we pointed at the least poisonous-looking potful. An overly-generous serving was then slopped messily into our plates.

Holding our pungent trays at arms length, we walked past our fellow-diners in this typical Soviet workers' eating place. Our beaming host had picked out a table for us. It was distinguished less for its cleanness than for its suitably remote location, which would make it easier to converse freely. We sat down; he prayed, and we began our unequal struggle with the food.

The conversation more than made up for any deficiency in the meal. This newly-discovered relative had spent six years in exile, in far-northern Vorkuta. Physically weak, he would undoubtedly have perished from the virtual slave-labor conditions and the paralyzing cold. His knowledge of the German language, however, made him useful to camp officials, and he was given indoor work as a translator.

Presently he was translating Christian literature from the German. Because he could type very fast, he was also responsible for producing copies of various kinds of Russian Christian publications. In fact, when we mentioned a booklet describing Pastor Robert Fetler's arrest and death, he smiled broadly and announced that that was one of his efforts.

"I have distributed that booklet from Kaliningrad in the West to Vladivostok in the East," he declared.

He nodded in recognition as we referred to the dictator of the prison camp. This was the nickname of an imprisoned pastor whose unshakable faith and moral strength had won him virtual control over hundreds of political prisoners and hardened criminals.

"Yes," he sighed, "thousands of our brethren suffered victorious martyrdom. This was the price paid for spreading the gospel message throughout Siberia. As a matter of fact," he added very quietly, looking around at those within earshot, "there's a book which we would very much like to get out and have published in the West. It consists of three volumes, the recollections of a Christian doctor, giving a detailed documented account of what our brethren endured during the Stalin era."

We walked the short distance back to the church, arriving just in time for the afternoon service. The visiting niece, Valya, was there, a pleasant-faced blonde, smartly dressed in a black and white striped suit. Also able to type very fast, she was of considerable help both to her pastor-father and her widely-travelled uncle. Our meeting was shortened by the fact that we both had other appointments, but she offered to walk with us to the tram stop to prolong the conversation for a few minutes.

No sooner had we started down the street than Valya was hailed by a young man who had also just left the church. We were introduced to him as Christian relatives from Canada and he to us as a member of the church choir.

"Will you be long?" he asked Valya anxiously.

"No," she replied, "just a few minutes."

"Good," he answered, "because brother Gregory from Tashkent wants to talk to you about something very important."

Here was another glimpse into the operation of that marvellous Christian communication network. Moscow was linked with the Ural mountains and Tashkent in Central Asia, almost two thousand miles from the Soviet capital, in a joint literature distribution project. In Leningrad we had heard of concerned Christian brethren who travelled five hundred miles north to Archangel, bringing aid and encouragement to a pastor who had been threatened with having his children placed in a state boarding school. In Kiev it would be a visitor reporting on church and prison conditions in Eastern Siberia, six thousand miles away.

We tried to reconcile conflicting impressions. Undoubtedly the Moscow church was something of a showplace, but we could not fault the preaching of the gospel which we had heard at the two services. The display of Soviet propaganda booklets in the visitors' area was distressing. The discovery that some of the members of this same Moscow church were involved in unofficial distribution of Christian literature was heartening. Pastor Zhidkov and other leaders did seem to be going too far to maintain a smooth relationship with government officials. Was that too high a price to pay for the privilege of holding six services a week in the central and fourteen suburban churches, with their combined membership of about 10,000? Compromises were being made, but what was their precise nature and significance? We would talk about the problem privately with believers in many churches. None of them could give us precise, unequivocal answers. None would care to estimate the proportions of the damage to/protection of believers which resulted from these actions of their leaders.

The central Moscow Baptist church was the one most visited by foreigners. As a showplace of the Soviet Union's alleged religious liberty, it should have provided the greatest opportunity for free contacts between its members and foreign Christians. But several visits to the church, identifying myself as both an academic exchange fellow and Baptist pastor, resulted only in a few polite comments from a couple of the preaching brethren. Our only contact with Pastor Zhidkov was an accidental, ten-second exchange as we moved in opposite directions.

"I felt like an orphan," I reported to Lil as I returned to our hotel one night. She had been ill and unable to attend the weeknight service. I had gone to the church directly from a long day's work at the library, stopping for a quick lunch at a tolerable stand-up snack bar.

Following the service I had made my way out of the balcony, exchanging greetings with a number of people.

They smiled and quickly moved on. As the crowd of worshippers streamed out into the street they formed into groups of half a dozen or so, talking and laughing together. As usual, I stood for several minutes in an open spot, waiting for someone to approach me. On one occasion an earnest BeloRussian woman had come up, shared her testimony of salvation, and asked for our prayers. Perhaps this time it would be someone like the young man who had told us how he obtained a Bible. Following his conversion he had walked the streets of Moscow, asking anyone who would listen to him if they could get him a Bible. He finally got one in the black market for 150 rubles ($240 Canadian) – a month's wages. I waited expectantly.

Within minutes, even though I was standing only a few yards from fellow-believers, I began to feel physically and spiritually all alone. After about a quarter of an hour a rather frightened-looking man, about fifty years old, sidled up to me. Obviously very nervous, he asked who I was. My reply brought forth a few stammering words of welcome and a parting "I must go now." No one else came up and I made my dejected way back to the hotel.

A few days later we found out that several of the members of the Moscow church had been arrested. The charge: undue fraternization with foreigners.

The news from the embassy was discouraging. Apparently my meeting with Professor Lialina, a leading specialist on Russian Baptists, could not take place after all. She had just received word of an important trip to another city in the USSR which could not be postponed. Furthermore, it was unlikely that she would be back before Professor Nesdoly would be leaving Moscow. For that matter, they had been expecting Professor Nesdoly to come the previous year, and arrangements had been made for a number of contacts with Soviet scholars at that time.

We had indeed planned to go in 1977, having completed all the preliminaries with the exception of one thing: final authorization from the appropriate Soviet authorities. Repeated checking with the Canada Council, which administers the exchange program, had resulted in repetition of the distressingly familiar plaint: "Nothing further from the Soviet end." The long-awaited authorization finally arrived, only a few days before I was scheduled to begin teaching again in September. Fortunately, the Soviet authorities had at least agreed to let me postpone the trip until 1978.

Another disappointment was waiting for me when I got to the library. I went directly to the microfilming department, expecting to pick up my substantial order. The clerk informed me curtly that it could not be filled. As patiently as I could, I explained to the now frightened clerk that I had specifically requested access to these materials in my application for acceptance as an exchange scholar. In granting permission to come, Soviet authorities had said nothing about objections to the sources which I had asked to examine. They were all pre-Revolutionary, dealing with Russian Baptist history. Obviously they had nothing to do with security-related topics.

The clerk was apologetic but unyielding, muttering something about old books that might be damaged by microfilming. She kept answering my questions on the reason for this refusal with a pathetic "I don't know. I don't know." Departmental and other supervisors were duly produced on my request to speak to someone who might give me a different answer. In each instance of ascending authority the answer was the same: "I'm sorry sir, but we cannot microfilm this material."

Finally I asked to see the head of the international section, a plump, businesslike woman in her forties whom I had met briefly on arrival at the library. In response to my complaints, she gave me a ritual speech about the worldwide exchange program of the Lenin Library – the largest in the world, she reminded me smugly. My own minor problems, she assured me, would be rectified immediately. Now, if that was all I had come for, she really must be getting back to her work.

Given my overall experience with the Soviet bureaucracy, I was not optimistic that anything would be done before we left Moscow. After ten years of trying to find materials, I could not get them duplicated. And I would certainly not have enough time to do all the reading involved.

When I arrived at the microfilming department a couple of days later, all had changed. The once pathetic, frightened clerk was all smiles and enthusiasm.

"We'll film all of it, sir! Everything, everything!" she announced, even before I could ask. Then, in an undertone, she added confidentially, "And we don't microfilm this kind of book for our own scholars, you know!"

More than a little heartened by this unexpectedly favourable and rapid resolution of my research problem, I felt somewhat freer to join Lil for some sightseeing. The days passed rapidly, with mornings generally spent in the library, afternoons in visiting various tourist attractions, and evenings at concerts or church activities.

My knowledge of Russian and Soviet history enabled me to spot some notable omissions and distortions in several museums. I could not resist asking tour guides and attendants some questions. Why, for example, was there no reference to Comrade Inessa Armand (reputedly Lenin's mistress), with whom he had corresponded extensively and whose death had affected him so profoundly? Why was there no mention of Comrade Roman Malinovsky, sponsored by the infallible revolutionary leader, Lenin, for many key positions and later revealed to be a longtime tsarist secret police agent? Most shocking of all was the total absence of any reference to Bronstein.

Up to this point, the guide had been mildly embarrassed. Now she looked puzzled and a bit apprehensive.

"Bronstein?" she asked.

"Yes," I replied, "the man who was probably the most prominent leader during the Revolution of 1905. He was Lenin's close associate, Chairman of the Petrograd Soviet and its Military Revolutionary Committee in 1917. Along with Lenin, he was the maker of the Bolshevik Revolution and creator of the Red Army. You probably know him better as Trotsky."

She looked at me disdainfully. "Trotsky! You didn't expect to find *him* here?"

Lenin, of course, was not only here, but everywhere. We were struck by the quasi-religious atmosphere in one museum. Stained-glass windows honored the creator of the USSR. Bouquets of fresh flowers had been placed reverently before the various portraits and busts. Solemn music and suitably dimmed lights added to the cathedral-like atmosphere. And to complete the picture, incense – in the form of the odor of cooking cabbage wafting up from the basement lunch counter. We decided not to join the long daily queues of faithful pilgrims who lined up in front of the Lenin Mausoleum in Red Square and waited patiently to see the mummified remains of this Communist creator-saint. Deification appeared in the form of a triple slogan painted on an inside wall of the Moscow Circus: "Lenin lived! Lenin lives! Lenin shall live!"

The circus was delightful, complete with the obviously impossible performances of gymnasts, aerialists, and illusionists. The various animal acts, particularly the world-famous bears, were superb. The clowns' pantomimes were hilarious. We had driven some four hundred miles, several years previously, to catch a performance in Calgary, Alberta. Now, a few minutes ride on the subway offered us the choice of the circus, the incredible skills of the Obratsov puppeteers, a symphony concert or opera performance at the Kremlin auditorium or in the magnificent Bolshoi Theater. Reasonably good seats could be had for about three dollars each, and we once managed to get upper balcony seats for an opera at the Bolshoi Theater for $1.30 apiece.

We'd had an interesting conversation with a Soviet bureaucrat on our way to the circus. In the course of our conversation, we discovered that he was a Ukrainian working for some government department in Moscow.

"Tell our Ukrainians in Canada that we are living well

here in the homeland," he suggested as we approached the circus stop.

"Ukrainians in Canada are also living very well," we assured him.

"But," he countered, "we have free medical service here."

"And Canada also has a state medical insurance system," we interjected.

"I know that. I also know that you have to pay very high premiums!"

"Even those provinces which do charge premiums don't charge much," we retorted. "And in some provinces we pay no premiums at all."

"Say whatever you want," he declared with finality, "but I know better!"

The young man lounging near a large black limousine in front of the Brazilian embassy was presumably somewhat less brainwashed. Lil had struck up a conversation with him as she passed by on the street. He expressed warm interest on discovering that she was here on a visit from Canada, and asked her how life there compared with what she had seen in the USSR. His interest continued as she got on to the subject of religion and the church, and he responded favourably to her invitation to attend the Baptist church sometime. It turned out that he had even been there on one previous occasion. The tract offered to him was also gratefully received. Waving a cheery goodbye he announced that it was time to pick up his boss, a senior official from the Kremlin.

At the time that we were in Moscow, another Canadian citizen was having some very painful experiences with the Brezhnev régime. We had heard about the incident during an interview with Ambassador Ford, at the embassy. In fact, he had to cut the interview short because of an urgent meeting with Soviet officials on the case in question; thus, the details were provided by one of the department officers.

A former Soviet citizen, of German extraction, the Canadian in question had left the USSR with the retreating German army in 1943. After a period in various displaced-persons camps, she had managed to emigrate to Canada, escaping the forcible repatriation of thousands of other Soviet citizens. Thirty-five years later she had returned to her home village for a visit. The emotional outpouring which accompanied her reunion with surviving relatives had overwhelmed her good judgment. Family keepsakes and heirlooms were showered upon her, including various gold and silver items and antique icons.

Just prior to her departure from the Moscow airport she had to pass through customs. She was asked if she had anything to declare and, not having purchased anything, she answered negatively. A search of her luggage revealed the family gifts. Where were the official papers, indicating that she had paid the export duty and thus had permission to remove these items from the USSR? Of course she had none. Her protests that these were gifts were brushed aside, as were her pleas that she simply must get on the departing plane.

She was arrested and jailed, held for six months before coming to trial. The charge was serious: attempting to smuggle out prohibited goods to the value of 33,000 rubles (over $50,000 Cdn. at the official exchange rate). A zealous prosecuting attorney demanded exemplary punishment in the form of a ten-year prison sentence. The more humane judge finally decided to reduce this to eight.

"Hopefully," said Marion as we talked about it on the way over to supper with our Singaporean friends, "Ambassador Ford will be able to persuade Soviet authorities to let her off with a heavy fine." Turning to

Jim, lounging comfortably in the front passenger seat, she warned him to be careful about what he bought. She had no intention of bailing him out of a Soviet jail.

Thanks to our hosts' cooking skills (and the excellent foodstuffs brought to Moscow on regular Singapore Airlines flights), the meal was superb. Afterwards, the physical feasting was followed by the spiritual. Different denominational backgrounds made for different insights as we studied the Scriptures together. And we did remember to speak loudly and clearly for the benefit of unseen listeners.

The evening concluded with a rousing hymn sing. Our hosts' musical abilities were as good as their cooking. Excellent pianists and near-professional singers, they provided the soprano and tenor sections. Lil and Marion filled in the alto and I growled a bass. Jim sang vigorously until Marion made him an offer he could not refuse. If he promised to stop singing, Marion promised to get him a couple of hamburgers later that evening.

13: Of Post-Offices and Politics

"Just a bit different from the way they do it in Canada, isn't it?" my queue companion laughed. He was another exchange scholar staying in the University Hotel and, like ourselves, wanting to mail a parcel back home. The procedure, it seems was to bring the article to the post office unwrapped. Presumably, having the postal clerks do the wrapping ensures that the state requirements are met. It also saves the authorities the time and trouble of opening parcels to check on their contents.

Parcels sent from the West sometimes fail to arrive. On other occasions the recipients may be required to pay a stiff import duty, with levels established arbitrarily by Soviet authorities. One family to whom we sent a parcel, including a highly-prized pair of blue jeans, told us simply, "Please do not send us any more parcels. We ended up having to buy the goods you sent – at official prices."

Another parcel which we sent was eventually returned to us in Canada, stamped as containing illegal goods. Fortunately, our local post office had a list of these forbidden goods. No, we had not been mistaken in our deciphering of the Russian words scrawled on the returned parcel. There, in a list including such things as narcotics, airplane parts, and machine guns, was the name of the offending product – chewing gum.

Letters are frequently opened, then crudely re-sealed with the Soviet equivalent of scotch tape or with generous smearings of a peculiar, thick brown glue. Occasionally, a more mechanically-minded censor will staple the ripped open envelope. Of course, some letters simply disappear. A second cousin of mine, puzzled about the sudden stoppage of regular letters from my father, spoke about this to fellow-villagers. Eventually the mystery was at least partly cleared up. The letters themselves were never found, but an empty envelope was discovered in the local graveyard.

Faced with these problems, letter writers have devised ingenious means of foiling the censors. One employee at the British embassy, for example, wrote letters to his mother in Welsh, a language apparently not within the censors' competence. Summoned to an official's office one day, he was surprised to find his opened letter lying on a desk. Asked to translate, he read smoothly, informing his mother of how wonderfully he was getting along in this marvellous city and asking innocent questions pertaining to family matters back in Wales.

A Canadian friend, anxious to avoid having to stay in Intourist hotels, wrote several letters to a relative in the USSR who had previously visited Canada. In each letter, he mentioned how pleasant it had been to have this relative stay in his home, rather than in a hotel. He then expressed the hope that he would have the same privilege during his forthcoming visit to the USSR. It was granted. Another Canadian visitor decided that sending a simple family picture back to Canada from his home village in the USSR would tell the whole story. If conditions were good, the Canadian tourist would be standing, if bad, he would be seated. The letter duly arrived with an enclosed picture – showing the Canadian visitor lying on the ground.

"And today," I said to Lil as we started out on the now-familiar bus and subway trip downtown, "we'll be getting a look at the place from which the whole Soviet system is controlled – the Kremlin." Guidebook at the ready, we walked the short distance from the subway stop, pausing to take a few panoramic shots of this walled-in cluster of Byzantine churches and more modern-looking government office buildings between Red Square and the Moskva river.

Here, as in Leningrad, we were impressed with the painstaking, spare-no-expense restorations of national treasures, particularly the old churches with their gold-coloured domes, topped with the distinctive Orthodox crosses. The Russian gigantomania was represented by *Tsar Pushka*, the world's largest cannon (never fired) and *Tsar Kolokol*, the world's largest bell (never rung), a small fragment of which weighs four tons. A guided tour through the heavily-guarded Armoury Museum left us breathless. Huge gold nuggets and massive chunks of platinum reminded us of the Soviet Union's leading status among the world's producers of precious metals. Crowns, sceptres, and elaborate tsarist court regalia sparkled with barbaric splendor as the light was reflected off egg-sized gemstones.

Earlier we had visited the assembly room of the Soviet Union's parliament. Known as the Supreme Soviet (Council), it consists of two houses, both elected by universal adult suffrage and by secret ballot. The Soviet of the Union is based on representation by population; the Soviet of Nationalities represents the different ethnic groups. The Supreme Soviet meets for a few days annually, presumably managing in that time to do all that any other government does besides making the basic decisions related to a completely state-owned economy.

Elections result in a participation rate of just a fraction less than 100%. The winning candidates always get a similarly impressive percentage of the votes cast. Westerners may find all of this a bit surprising, considering that the only choice which the voter has is to vote yes or no to the single name on the ballot.

According to the guidebook, there was a former private chapel and a restored typical middle-class sixteenth-century home near the Hotel Rossiia. There would be just enough time left for a quick tour and another look through the hotel's foreign currency shop. Perhaps we would still be able to find the German or Japanese tape recorder that Anton wanted.

Five centuries of architectural experimentation blended inharmoniously around us. The red and white Byzantine family chapel, dating from the sixteenth century, could have accommodated a few hundred worshippers, rather than the dozen or so sightseers who were following the middle-aged guide. Extremely knowledgeable in Biblical history, she dwelt in considerable detail, for example, on the incident portrayed in the painting of Saul of Tarsus on the Damascus road. From the warmth and urgency of her tone, she seemed to be engaged in evangelism rather than officially-correct, detached explanation.

When the tour was over and the others had left, Lil and I stayed behind to express our appreciation. The guide smiled warmly as we thanked her for the personal conviction which seemed to permeate her words. She shook her head negatively as I reached into my inside coat pocket, perhaps thinking that I was going to offer her a tip. But her face absolutely glowed and she uttered a heartfelt "God be with you!" as she took the Russian tract.

14: Of Purchases, Prayers, and Persecution

The foreign-currency shop was especially well-stocked. A surprising item was the display of little bottles of that very capitalist drink, Pepsi-Cola, complete with labels printed in Russian. More important, the shop had a combination radio-tape recorder made by Sony. We cashed a couple of travellers' cheques, paid the 120 rubles ($192 Canadian) and headed for the subway station.

We had walked no more than a block when two swarthy-looking men in their thirties came running up to ask where we had bought the tape recorder. On hearing that it was in the foreign-currency shop, their faces fell.

"And how much did you pay?" one of them asked.

My reply, "120 rubles," triggered off an alternating chorus of escalating bids and my own steady refusal to sell. The bidding stopped at 500 rubles. Why was I being so stubborn?

They could not go into the foreign-currency stores and high-quality goods such as this tape recorder were simply not available to ordinary citizens. "Just for the big guys," one of them snorted. My protests that we had no use for the extra rubles and that these could certainly not be converted into Western currency when we left were met with blank stares. Mentioning that I had bought the tape recorder for a friend produced a more understanding, even sympathetic look.

"Well, then," one of the Armenian entrepreneurs suggested, "I have an easy solution. Sell us the tape recorder for 500 rubles and give the unused rubles to your Russian friend. He can certainly make use of them. Then go and buy him another tape recorder at the same store. They don't care how many you buy!"

Not wanting to run the risk of losing the Japanese tape recorder we had finally been able to buy (and then discover that there were no more available) I once again refused. Presumably thinking that he had encountered an incredibly sharp bargainer, the more persistent trader made his final offer.

"Five hundred rubles and, for you, my friend, what is easily worth another five hundred – my solid gold ring," he said grandly.

Expressing our admiration for the Armenians' well-deserved reputation as traders, we went on our way. Privately, we wondered about the Russian proverb that says: "When you've shaken hands with an Armenian, count your fingers." We watched the two of them walking off dejectedly, presumably amazed that supposedly capitalistic Westerners should act in such an un-capitalistic way.

"Buying gifts for friends is one thing," I said to Lil as we approached the subway station, "but we don't want to get involved in the kind of illegal business that those two were suggesting. Reminds me of the two young men in Leningrad who offered me rubles at half the official rate and then, when I refused, asked if I'd like to buy some antique icons. By the way, is this the station where you met Elizaveta?" I asked as we started down the escalator.

"I think it was closer to Gorky Street, near that restaurant where I almost ate the caviar," Lil replied.

Elizaveta, a pretty seventeen-year-old, had come up to Lil in the subway station, greeting her with a warm, "I saw you at church yesterday." She was on her way to GUM (the State Department Store) to buy an umbrella.

Lil suggested that they should check out a nearby foreign-currency shop. Elizaveta was delighted, having heard of, but never having visited such a place.

Lil was just as delighted to observe the girl's reactions when they walked past the glowering doorman and into this shoppers' paradise. She was like a child turned loose in a fantastic toystore: head swivelling, mouth agape, blue eyes sparkling in wonder. After a few minutes of this awe-struck general survey, she followed Lil to a counter presided over by a rather stony-faced clerk.

"We'd like to see your umbrellas," Lil said politely. "The automatic ones, please."

Elizaveta looked at the pile of foreign-made umbrellas ecstatically. She scarcely knew what to make of this unheard-of selection of colours, to say nothing of the unheard-of opportunity to try them out. Why, she could actually push the open button and watch wide-eyed as the umbrella unfurled all by itself.

"Take your time, my dear," Lil advised. "Try as many as you like before picking out the one you want. I'm sure the clerk won't mind."

After several automatics had been tried and handed back to the simmering clerk to repack, Elizaveta finally selected one. The price was seven rubles. An inferior-quality one, if available at all in GUM, would have cost forty-nine.

"You must come and visit my mother," said Elizaveta excitedly when they were back out on the street again. Lil was reluctant to do so, remembering the problems experienced by some Moscow Baptists for fraternizing with foreigners. But Elizaveta insisted, and so they went, by subway and then by bus, to an apartment in the surburbs.

"God has sent you here today," said the plump, shiny-faced woman who came to the door. "Come in, come in. We'll have a bite to eat and share some Christian fellowship." Over tea and delicious pancakes with a choice of home-made jam or honey, they talked, read the Scriptures, laughed, wept, and prayed together. Mother was a long-time Christian and member of the Moscow Baptist church. Elizaveta had been converted only one year ago. Both had been threatened with death many times by the father, a terrible drunkard. Now they were rejoicing in God's mercy. The father was still coming home badly intoxicated, but he was no longer threatening to kill them; thus, they no longer had to hide the kitchen knives every night.

It was all very perplexing and very humbling. By Western standards they were materially poor. But, unlike many Western Christians, they were content – even happy. If the dominant note in Western prayers seemed to be, "Lord, give," among these believers it was, "Thank you, Lord." Here, persecution was accompanied by praise. In the West, comfortableness bred complacency and complaint. Undoubtedly there are also Russian Christians who are no more spiritually alive than the average Western church-goer, but they must be in the minority. The hundreds whom we met at twenty-eight services in eight different churches or in their homes seemed to be more like Elizaveta and her mother. They were ordinary people living extraordinary Christian lives under extremely difficult conditions.

In the USSR, official and social opposition means that any identification with Christianity is costly. Yet many are prepared to pay the price and the church is growing. In the West, governments actually aid the churches through tax concessions and church attendance is still considered to be socially respectable. Despite these advantages, overall, church attendance is steadily dropping.

In some Western churches the former doctrinal rigor has been compromised and the former demanding, separatist life-style membership requirements have been relaxed. The results, it seems, have been uniformly bad. Despite the concessions, some of these same churches have actually *lost* members. Others have grown in the number of those attending the Sunday morning service, in full-time salaried staff, and in both size and luxury of the church plant, as the building is sometimes appropriately called. But size and splendor do not necessarily mean spiritual strength.

In the USSR, our careful observation and questioning confirmed the impressions gained through extensive reading and research. The Russian Baptists know neither theological nor moral liberalism. Reform Baptist leader Georgi Vins, for example, shortly after his arrival (1979) in the United States was asked to give his impressions of North American Christianity. He was very tactful, insisting that a guest does not criticize his host's ways. Noting the denial of Biblical inspiration in some Baptist seminaries, however, he observed that, thank God, the Russian Baptists had never had such a problem. Had they tolerated liberalism, he added, there would be no Russian Baptist movement today.

The general stance of Russian Baptists on a separated lifestyle can be summarized in the words of one of the preaching brethren in a large Union church in the USSR, who unhesitatingly identified himself as a fundamentalist. He also spoke to his young wife about modesty, though her very high-necked blouse was opened a bare inch at the top. Shocked by our report of the growing acceptance of social drinking by Western evangelicals, a preacher in an Independent church assured me that *all* Russian Baptists "at least keep themselves from such things." He added that any church member who touched alcoholic beverages would be visited immediately by the preaching brethren. If he did not repent, his name would be read from the pulpit and none of the members would have any fellow-ship with him until he changed his ways.

In general, it seems that all Baptist churches in the USSR set high spiritual and moral standards for their members. Pastoral watchfulness and general congregational support and encouragement help to ensure that these standards will be observed in daily living. Admittedly, the watchfulness and encouragement may occasionally be out of proportion to the size of the issues involved. Concern for truth and purity may sometimes become mixed with personality and taste differences, producing unnecessary and un-Christian conflict. Yet the zeal for truth and purity is surely understandable. After all, surely a very high level of spiritual and moral excellence is demanded of those who would take their Christianity seriously. How else can one endeavor to live up to truly Biblical standards, or carry on the unrelenting struggle with the world – whether Western or atheist-communist – that knows not God?

Baptists in the USSR do stand out from their fellow-citizens in terms of standards and life-style. They are rigorously honest in a land where lying seems to be a national disease and in which, as we were told, one almost has to steal in order to live. Their diligence as workers stands in marked contrast with the performance of so many in the Soviet workforce, whose goal seems to be to ensure that no one does less work than they do. Noting the changed lives of former drunkards who join the Baptists, some Soviet officials have suggested to Baptist leaders that they should really stick to this socially-useful rehabilitation work, instead of wasting their time in preaching this religious nonsense!

In the course of her sightseeing during our last week in Moscow, Lil made a special point of inviting various people to services at the Baptist church. Responses ranged from warmly-enthusiastic to very hostile. In the latter category, of particular interest, were the incredulous replies of two separate women: "Go to the Baptist church! Don't you know that the Baptists actually offer up their own children as bloody sacrifices to their 'god'?"

Despite official and social opposition and smear-tactics such as these, the Baptist churches, in Moscow and elsewhere, continue to attract new converts. We were sitting in our customary balcony position during a Sunday evening service. I had done some rough translating of the first speaker's message for a handsome black man in an impressive-looking uniform. He was an Ethiopian army officer, in Moscow for special military training. He was also an evangelical Christian, acquainted with the medical missionary work done by close friends of ours from a Baptist church in Western Canada.

Lil had been able to overhear a whispered conversation between a couple, seated diagonally behind her, three rows higher up in the balcony.

"I must go and talk to one of the preachers," the wife said to her husband, having listened intently to the choir's stirring anthem and the first speaker's urgent gospel message. She rose to leave.

"There'll be time to do that at the end of the service," her husband replied. "Sit down."

She sat down reluctantly. "But maybe I'll forget by the time the service ends," she protested.

"If God is really speaking to you, you won't forget," he answered. "Shh! The choir is going to sing again. Listen."

The choir sang. The second speaker had just begun his message when the wife's voice – half-sob, half-whisper – was heard again. "I can't wait any longer. I must go immediately and speak to someone about my sinful soul!"

There were no protests from her husband as she moved quickly from her seat. She squeezed past some glowing-faced sisters who were whispering "Glory to God!" Half-running down the stairs, she disappeared into a prayer/counselling room under the platform.

"Quite a showplace, this Moscow church," said a gaunt, shabbily-dressed man, coming up to us in the street after a Sunday morning service.

"Yes," I agreed, introducing Lil and myself as Christians from Canada and adding that we realized that not all churches in the USSR were functioning as freely as this one.

"Just last week, in Rostov," he said quietly, "the police cracked down on us again. Practically all of us church members were arrested and jailed. We were crammed together so tightly in our cells that we had to sleep sitting on the floor, with knees drawn up to our bowed heads." Then, breaking into a toothless grin, he added, "But we prayed and sang hymns together, and as we did so, the jailers applauded and asked for more.

"This kind of persecution has been going on for a very long time," he continued, his voice breaking. "Forgive me," he whispered, as he tried to regain his composure, "but you will understand that I cannot speak dispassionately (*ravnodushno*-literally, in an even-souled way) about these matters. Our dear pastor is only thirty-six years old. He was first arrested at age eighteen, and thus he has known alternating imprisonment and release for half his life. He has eight children, and this time his pregnant wife was also jailed."

We stood there together in the street as Pastor Zhidkov and some visiting American Baptists got into a couple of cars and drove off. The other 2,000 Sunday morning worshippers, having visited briefly in the street, were making their way to the tram stop. As we walked along, our new friend informed us that undoubtedly the pastor and other leading brethren of the Rostov church could tell us more. "But," he concluded humbly, "I'm just one of the ordinary members."

"Well," I said, blinking back the tears, "here's something to help the persecuted brethren. It comes from the persecutors," I added, explaining that it was part of my living-expense allowance from the Soviet government.

He tucked the fifty-ruble bill carefully into an inside pocket, thanking us almost reverently on behalf of his fellow-sufferers. With a glorious smile illuminating his creased, white-stubbled face, he whispered a fervent "*Bog s vami!*" (God be with you!) as we shared a farewell embrace. From his window seat on the fast-disappearing tram he waved goodbye, hands clasped above his head in a triumphant victory salute.

15: *Things Old and New*

Our checking-out experience in Leningrad had taught me not to leave things to the last minute and we were confident that all arrangements had been made three days before our departure for Kiev. Unfortunately, there seemed to be a communication gap between a couple of government departments, but a quick trip to the nearby office easily cleared up the problem. The University of Leningrad had finally completed the arrangements for our stay in Kiev. On arrival in the Ukraine's capital city we would be met by a driver from the Academy of Sciences. We were to stay at the Libid (Swan) Hotel.

Having arrived at the railway station some two hours before our scheduled 8:30 p.m. departure for Kiev, we had time to watch a kind of capsule portrayal of the 100 different peoples living in the USSR. Balts, Belo-Russians, Great Russians and Ukrainians made up the European segment. There were also Georgians, Armenians, and Azerbaijanis, whose homeland in the Caucasus is a veritable ethnographic museum, marking the transition from Europe to Asia. We moved carefully past the skull-capped Uzbeks from romantic, ancient Central Asian cities such as Bokhara and Samarkand. That care arose from our memory of the unromantic, if ever so delicate ways in which some of these men spat in the streets. A dozen or so Kazakhs, Kirgiz, and Turkmenians stood guarding the mounds of goods purchased in Moscow. Descendants of nomadic steppe-land horsemen, they looked strangely out of place, dressed in their ill-fitting, mismatched "suits" and standing in a crowded Moscow railway station. So did the few Mongol people, whose remote ancestors rode with the armies of Genghis Khan.

We boarded the train for the overnight trip to Kiev, sharing our compartment with a well-dressed young mother and her chubby youngster. The time passed pleasantly as we sampled one another's travel lunches and exchanged classroom gossip with this schoolteacher. Perhaps her unresponsiveness to the gospel was related to the children's book which she was reading to her son. Very attractively printed, with full-color illustrations, it told about a wonderful man. He had freed Russia from the cruel yoke of tsars and landlords, thereby bringing untold blessings to the children of the USSR and the entire world. The semi-divine leader was, of course, Lenin – Little Grandfather Lenin, to be more precise. The mother's dramatic reading, combined with what we could see of the illustrations, recalled the quasi-religious atmosphere of the Lenin Museum.

An attendant had arrived with blankets and pillows, enabling us to make up our soft-class sleeping accommodation. The long twilight faded into night as we rattled along southward, dozing intermittently. We awoke to brilliant morning sunshine flooding through the closed windows of our already too-warm compartment. Stretching our cramped limbs we made our way out into the corridor running along one side of the railway car.

The countryside looked strangely familiar. Broad green fields, dotted here and there with clumps of trees, stretched out for mile after mile toward the distant horizon. It looked so very much like Saskatchewan. Along with so many other European immigrants to Canada, our ancestors had chosen to settle in that part of the new homeland which was most like the old.

As we passed rapidly through an occasional village we caught a glimpse of lush-looking gardens behind white-washed fences and ablaze with well-tended flower beds. A word, a gesture, a murmured "Mmmmm!" – years of travelling together meant that we did not have to say much. Lil and I looked at one another and smiled. We had the most peculiar feeling of having come home.

The train pulled into the railway station and we trundled our increasingly bulgy suitcases out on to the platform. There was the promised car and driver. A short ride to the yellow stucco Academy of Sciences building was followed by a similarly short meeting with a pleasantly efficient administrator. We were delighted, if a bit skeptical, when he assured us that getting visas to visit our ancestral village would pose no problem. He would need our passports, the name of a contact person in the village, and the dates of our proposed visit. The paper work might take a couple of days at most.

The pretty blonde clerk at the Libid Hotel's front desk had our registration checked in a minute. Still rather dazed from our long train ride and the surprisingly quick settling of research, travel, and hotel business we were ushered into a very clean, comfortable room on the fifth floor. A refreshing soak in the deep tub and we were ready to begin the day. After all, as Lil observed, we had already been in Kiev for over an hour.

We had promised a Canadian friend that we would 'phone his brother in Kiev. His wife answered my call, informing me that Petro was at work, but that she would get him to call us at the hotel. Fifteen minutes later there was a knock at the door. A short, smiling man in his mid-fifties identified himself as Petro and insisted that we come along to his apartment for lunch immediately.

"But what about your work?", Lil and I chorused, noting that it was only mid-morning.

"We Ukrainians have a saying that work is not like a wolf. It won't run away," he laughed.

Gathering up the gifts which his brother had given us to pass on to him, we followed Petro out to his little red Zaporozhets. Once again there was something very familiar about our conversation. The tone, the quirks of expression, the delightfully natural sense of humor were indistinguishable from those of his Canadian brother.

That impression was strengthened as we drove toward Petro's apartment and he told us about how he had been tragically separated from the rest of his family. "I was a Red Army soldier on the Leningrad front," he began, "when the Soviet bomb fell on our home here in German-occupied Kiev. Two brothers, a sister and my mother were killed. Father, himself badly wounded, held mother's hand and prayed with her as her life ebbed away. As my brother Stepan probably told you," he continued, "the blast blew him into a lean-to goat shed. Another sister, visiting friends at the time, also escaped death.

"In due time the Soviet armed forces liberated the city, finding only about one-tenth of the almost one million people who lived here in 1941 when the Germans had invaded. All the surviving members of my family were taken West by the retreating German forces. Praise God, they escaped the fate of so many others – death in a concentration camp – thanks to my sister's ability to speak German.

"Having lost part of my foot, I was discharged as an invalid," he went on, expertly guiding the car with combined foot and hand controls. "That's one of the reasons, by the way, that I have this car and other privileges. When I got back to Kiev, it was so devastated that I had difficulty getting my bearings at all. Finally, I found my way to our section of the city, but there was only a pile of rubble where our house had been. Worse still, none of the family could be found. It was some time before I could piece the story together from bits of contradictory information which various people gave me. At long last I established letter contact with the family in Canada and we corresponded for several years, looking forward to the time when we could see one another again.

"But here we are," he concluded, bringing his car to a stop in a small parking lot enclosed by apartment buildings. "The place where our house used to stand is just over there. You'll be able to see it better from our apartment," he explained, as we entered the elevator.

The apartment was somewhat larger than average, attractively-furnished and filled with the tantalizing smells of cooking food. Petro's wife, Anna, a tall handsome woman, welcomed us graciously. "Lunch will be ready in a little while," she said to her husband. "Let Lil stay here with me while you take Sam down to the market and see if you can get some nice strawberries."

The first strawberries of the season were predictably expensive at about $2.75 a pound. My suggestion that we check out some other stalls, where the berries might be a bit cheaper, was brushed aside. "So what if they're expensive – so long as they're good!" Nor would he hear of my paying for the berries. After all, was it not traditional that the Ukrainian would spend all he had to provide a feast for honoured guests?

This too was distressingly familiar. "I hope you're not going to be like your brother in Canada," I protested. "His refusal to let anyone else pay for anything has driven me to near-dishonesty on occasion."

Petro insisted innocently that he was really not like his brother in that way. He was also ready with another Ukrainian proverb: "If they give, take. If they beat, flee." Nodding repeatedly as the vendor dropped handful after handful of berries into a huge bag, Petro paid some horrendous amount and we headed back to the car.

The berries were scarcely needed, given the veritable banquet which Anna served. There was borshch, breads, tender cutlets and other meats, salads, several varieties of mushrooms, and a bewildering array of fancy baked goods. Anna apologized for feeding us these remnants of their son's recent birthday party, but promised us a prepared meal on another occasion. Minutes stretched unnoticed into hours as we talked and ate.

Petro continued his account of his attempts to get permission to visit the family in Canada, noting that this finally took place thirty-five years after they had been separated. "We had a wonderful reunion," he concluded, "marred only by the fact that my father had died a few years earlier."

"We met him a few times at your brother's place," I commented, "and found him to be much like my own father: steadfast in his Christian devotion and simply full of fascinating stories."

"Exactly my impression of your father," Petro answered. "My brother took me out for a wonderful visit with your parents. Your mother stuffed us with so many different kinds of food that we could hardly breathe!"

"That must be a basic characteristic of Ukrainian women," Lil and I laughed, glancing meaningfully at the still-loaded table. Predictably, Anna protested that we had scarcely touched anything. She insisted that at least we should let her pack us a bag of baked goods to take back to the hotel with us.

The 'phone rang a couple of times during our visit. Once it was their married daughter, Olena, checking about some family matter. Hearing that her parents had visitors from Canada, she insisted that we must come to her place for a meal the following Sunday. Another call was from someone who wanted Petro to fix his television set, having heard that he offered very much better service than was available at the few state-operated repair centres in this city of two million.

"Well," said Petro, returning to the table, "I told you that work will not run away. In addition to my pension as a war veteran, I have a job in the phonograph record plant where our son also works. By working steadily I can fill my quota in part of the time we are given; thus, I can take days off occasionally. If our son has to go to some place with the church young people's group, I can take over his quota for that day.

"As you might gather from the stereo items which you brought me from my brother, I'm also interested in TV, radios, and sound equipment. Word gets around that I can generally repair these things fairly quickly, in the person's own home. As a matter of fact," he laughed, "I look upon these repair visits mainly as opportunities to witness for Christ."

We asked about the church situation in Kiev, discovering that there are four Baptist Union churches and a Reform Baptist church in the city. The latter, probably the largest, is also a registered congregation and has a new building. "I'll take you there sometime, if you wish," Petro offered in response to our expressed interest in visiting this church, made famous by the activities of a well-known Reform Baptist leader, Georgi Vins.

Anna looked uneasy. "It breaks my heart," she half-sobbed, "to see what is going on. Some people from our own church, lifelong friends, in fact, have gone over there. Now, when we meet on the street, they won't even talk to us. And we haven't changed at all since we first knew them."

"Yes," Petro agreed, "there have been some very sad developments. But some of our members who left in anger to join the Reform church came back in repentance. I suppose there have been wrongs done on both sides and that sincere, dedicated Christians can have strong differences of opinion on this whole question of church-state relations."

"I'm reminded of what the late Brother Urban, long-time Russian evangelical pastor in Paris, once told me," I interjected. "He was at a Baptist convention, when an American state governor, the guest speaker, declared that he had discovered the origin of Baptists – back in the book of Genesis. Pressed for an explanation, he referred to the story of Abraham and Lot, where Abraham says, 'If you're going in that direction, I'm going in the opposite direction.' "

The earlier, more somber mood was further lightened by the arrival of their son. A tall, dark-haired young man in his early twenties, he was undoubtedly the envy of practically all his comtemporaries, dressed as he was in a complete Levi's outfit from his namesake uncle in Canada. Like his sister, he expressed his sincere joy at our visit.

"Perhaps, Mother," he suggested with slightly-feigned innocence, "now that Uncle Stepan's friends are here, we could take them to visit Odessa. We haven't visited our relatives there for a long time now."

She rumpled his thick hair affectionately. "It's not the relatives that he wants to see in Odessa," she explained. "You may know that Odessa has a reputation for being a city where you can buy things unavailable anywhere else. For a long time now he's been dying to get a pair of aviator-type sunglasses. So you see?", she trailed off, gesturing meaningfully.

He chuckled as he moved toward his room, wanting to get ready for a young people's gathering that evening. "They're always up to something," Anna observed nervously as she cleaned up the dishes. "Sometimes the young people are simply not careful with their activity. Church leaders are thus understandably concerned about our young people bringing down needless official repression upon us. In fact," she added as Stepan reappeared, "in some of our churches 'newly-converted' young people – probably highly-trained police agents – are pushing existing young people's groups to be extremely aggressive. Sooner or later they go too far and then the authorities have an excuse for arrests, fines, and so forth."

"You worry too much, Mother," said Stepan good-humoredly as he came back into the dining room. "We're not going anywhere special tonight, nothing like the visit a while back."

Intrigued, we asked for some details. He looked quickly at his watch, set down the home-made electric guitar and amplifer, and began his story.

"About thirty of us young people decided to take a little trip out to a fairly remote village, partly just to have an outing and partly to minister to two elderly believers who lived there. The sisters greeted us joyfully, and while they were getting a little lunch ready we began to sing, accompanied by the instruments which we had brought.

"Suddenly there was a loud knocking on the door. One of our fellows opened it and there stood a man who identified himself as the chairman of the local soviet and asked us what was going on. Taken aback, our spokesman informed him that we were Christian young people from Kiev who had come to visit these older sisters, and now we were having a little sing-song. Was there anything wrong with that?

" 'Why, this place is too small for all of you,' the chairman told him. 'Come down to the local clubhouse and then all the villagers can come and listen to your singing.'

"After an hour-long concert of singing, music, and recital of Christian poetry, we started back to Kiev. On the way back to the church we stopped to visit a branch of the Museum of the History of Religion and Atheism. If you've visited the one in Leningrad, you'll understand what this place was like.

"One of the most striking displays was a large glass case with several life-sized figures in it. According to the accompanying explanation, these wild-eyed people were Pentecostals engaged in some sort of frenzied, mystical religious orgy.

"I noticed that the display included a handwritten hymnal, open to a familiar hymn. So I called the others over to the case and we began to sing. In an instant we were surrounded by the entire museum staff. And you know," he concluded, grinning delightedly and sounding uncannily like his father and uncle, "even though we sang pretty well, in four-part harmony, for some reason the staff didn't seem to appreciate it!"

16: *Why Do They Think and Act That Way?*

We had slept late, exhausted from the long train ride and almost sleepless previous night. Breakfast in the hotel restaurant, though adequate, was a far cry from the food enjoyed with our friends. Overhearing an angry-sounding American trying to shout and swear an uncomprehending desk clerk into understanding his problem, we went over to do some translating. I explained to the newly-arrived tourist that Soviet hotel administration procedures could be slow and they were different. But they were not necessarily "incredibly stupid," as the American kept insisting.

The Canadian Ukrainians waiting to be checked in had a few problems, though the hotel clerks occasionally looked puzzled, hearing the native language interspersed with slightly Ukranianized, but basically English, words. We were reminded of the time in Moscow when we had asked a smartly-uniformed officer for directions to a museum, using the interrogative *chi*? (In this case, *which*?). Brightening, he had replied, in BBC English, "Oh, you are Ukrainians, from Canada."

Lil went off to get a general picture of the city and to visit whatever tourist attractions seemed interesting. I wanted to pick up my library passes and settle other research and travel matters, including a proposed week-end trip to Borodianka (the village from which our grandparents had migrated to Canada early in the century).

There was a large crowd in front of the hotel. Most of the people were talking excitedly, pointing to something in the ornamental bushes about fifty feet from the main entrance. Curious, I walked over, despite disapproving looks from some of the bystanders. There, in the midst of freshly-broken branches and a circle of randomly-scattered soil, was the body of a middle-aged man. He had just leaped from a seventeenth-storey window.

I began to walk rapidly down the beautiful, tree-lined streets leading to the Academy of Sciences. A majestic Orthodox cathedral, its bright blue walls and golden domes sparkling in the morning sun, was open. The gorgeously-decorated interior was certainly awesome in its size and richness. Hundreds of candles flickered in front of antique icons portraying the Virgin and Child or various saints. A scattering of worshippers, with a few exceptions mainly older women, moved from icon to icon, relic case to relic case, kneeling, kissing, crossing themselves, then moving on.

I remembered the semi-legendary account of how Christianity had come to Russia. Grand Prince Vladimir of Kiev had been investigating the claims of various religions. Islam was rejected because it prohibited wine, and "drinking was the Russians' joy." Judaism, in Vladimir's view, must have been abandoned by its God, for its followers had been driven out of their homeland. On visiting a Greek Orthodox cathedral, however, Vladimir's envoys had been overwhelmed by the decor, the magnificence of the richly-garbed priests and the elaborate ritual – so much so, that "they knew not whether they were on earth or in Heaven." Thus, impressed essentially by these external attributes, Vladimir had been baptized as an Orthodox believer in 988. Deciding for his pagan Slavic subjects he had compelled them to follow his example in being baptized en masse.

Officially, Russia was Christian, but more by command and coercion than by conversion. The pagan Slavs, according to one interpretation, gradually fused the new religion with the old. The teachings of Christianity were not really understood. Christian ritual was looked upon as essentially a better, because more powerful, form of magic, its effectiveness dependent upon scrupulously-accurate performance of ritual in every detail. Though many other factors were involved, the *Raskol* (Schism) in mid-seventeenth century, for example, had split Orthodoxy into two camps. Bitter controversy had raged over such things as the spelling of the name Jesus, the direction to be taken in church processions, and the number of fingers to be used in crossing oneself.

During its near-millennium of existence, Russian Orthodoxy had produced its own galaxy of talented theologians and preachers, pious monks and missionaries, saints canonized or common, devoted parish priests and devout parishioners. Orthodoxy had brought Russia its Cyrillic alphabet and its earliest high culture, in terms of literature, music, architecture, painting, and thought. It had left its indelible impact on the national mind, with its emphasis on oneness – the integration of all aspects of life by one single, all-embracing belief system. Part of the Orthodox heritage too was the Russians' sense of their peculiar relationship with the West: sharing a common Christian background, yet being different; converted to Christianity not by Rome, but by Constantinople. The eleventh-century schism separating Eastern and Western Christianity, together with the fall of Constantinople to the Ottoman Turks in 1453, had strengthened Russian Orthodoxy's conviction that it alone represented true Christianity. Moscow became the Third Rome, destined to carry on the great civilizing and Christianizing missions of the fallen Western and Eastern Roman Empires.

Interacting with other historical and cultural forces – the two-centuries long Mongol yoke, the absence of Renaissance and Reformation, the persistence of serfdom and autocracy – Orthodoxy thus contributed to the formation of a distinctive national mind. Thus, Soviet communism's emphasis on: authoritarian leadership and initiative from above; official adherence to a single belief system integrating all aspects of life. Its sense of being different from and superior to the West and of being destined to fulfil a great civilizing mission are not the products of Marxist-Leninist ideology alone. Rather, they also have deep roots in the Russian past.

History has apparently repeated itself. The medieval fusion of Slavic paganism and Greek Orthodoxy has its twentieth-century counterpart in the fusion of Russian Orthodoxy and Soviet Marxism. The result, thanks in part to the work of Lenin and the ex-seminarian, Stalin, has been a substitute religion, complete with dogma and hierarchy, shrines and ritual. Perhaps adherents of the new faith know its teachings better than Orthodox parishioners had once known theirs. But for most, it seems, their communist "religion" has become less a matter of living, life-changing belief and more a matter of performance of ritual and repetition of traditional expressions.

Interpreting the infallible Marxist scriptures, the aged patriarch and metropolitans in the Kremlin solemnly issue binding, all-fronts decrees. These are passed on and explained to the faithful by lower levels of the party priesthood. Communist holy days are celebrated with pomp and pageantry. Pious pilgrims visit museum-shrines or the most sacred place of all, the mausoleum of the demi-god, Lenin. In conversation with Soviet citizens one is struck with the repetition of stock phrases, slogans, labels – seemingly less understood than memorized.

For whatever reason, some loyal communists try to keep an occasional foot in the old Orthodox camp. They use the church for traditional marriages, infant baptisms, and burials. Grey Soviet life and garish Soviet holy days failing to satisfy their artistic and spiritual needs, these people still join the crowds in magnificent Orthodox cathedrals during special Christmas and Easter services. Others, in rural areas especially, retain one of the less-admirable features of traditional peasant religiosity. They insist on getting thoroughly drunk on all the old Orthodox church holidays.

Traditional language persists, even though the speaker is a die-hard atheist. A Canadian professor once met Khrushchev during a visit to the USSR. The Soviet leader remarked that, as a professor of philosophy, the Canadian must, of course, be an atheist. On being assured that the said professor was not only a believer but also an active Presbyterian layman, Khrushchev boasted that: "In our country, thank God, there is no God!"

Admittedly there is only so much that an atheist régime can do in its campaign against religion. Still, it must be galling for Soviet officials to have to continue to call the first day of the week by its unique Russian name – *Voskresenia* (Resurrection).

I had reached the Academy of Sciences building. Our passports were left to receive the appropriate visa stamps and I provided the name of my second cousin as a contact person. The polite official assured me that there should be no problem if we wanted a friend to drive us out there. Otherwise, we could take the electric train for a small charge – probably less than a ruble. Library passes in hand I went out into the street, thinking of how my in-laws had been required to travel to the village on their last visit to the USSR. They had been allowed to spend two hours in Borodianka, and they had to spend $150 (US) for the forty-minute trip by taxi.

I walked down the street to the university, admiring the park on my right and the profusion of rose bushes in full bloom. In the park, directly in front of the university, stood an impressive statue of the national hero of the Ukraine, Taras Shevchenko. Artist, musician, poet, patriot – he was the only character in Kiev who could even come close to Lenin, in terms of public recognition in the form of museums, buildings, and streets named after him.

The university was painted a garish red. According to popular legend, the colour goes back to a decision by the tsarist government. Angered by the ungratefulness of revolutionary students, some tsarist official decreed that the building should be painted red so that even if the students did not blush for shame, at least the building would do so.

In the course of waiting for a clerk to produce a requested catalogue, I was approached by a thirty-ish, scholarly-looking man. He identified himself as a language teacher who wanted to practise his pronunciation of various English words. Did I have a few minutes to spare? In the course of our conversation, he informed me quietly that he was hoping to get permission to emigrate. Hearing of my special research interests and personal Christian convictions he seemed delighted.

"Could we meet to discuss religious questions? I have so many things that I'd like to ask about," he asked.

I was prepared to go out to the park immediately, but he had some pressing business and we decided on four o'clock that afternoon. Unfortunately, he never showed up that day, nor did I see him again during the week or so that I spent in the university library. Perhaps the especially attentive library clerk had overheard our conversation. Perhaps that clerk was the library's equivalent of cousin Nikolai who, during my in-law's first visit to the village, had insisted on accompanying them on each and every call they made.

The experience of another Canadian visiting the Ukraine is also illuminating. She had brought along a prayer book to give to an aged aunt in her ancestral village. Searched at the border, she insisted that the book was for her personal use.

"Fine," said the customs officer, "just make sure that you still have the book when you return next week."

The woman was now faced with a dilemma. She could leave the book with her aunt and risk detention on her outbound trip. If she told her aunt that she had brought the book, but could not leave it, the old woman would be heartbroken. A fellow-traveller suggested helpfully that she should conceal the book and tell the aunt that she had indeed brought it, but that border officials had confiscated it.

When the tour group returned, the same customs officer was on duty. Coming up to the nervous traveller, he asked to see the prayer book, which she duly produced. Smiling politely, the officer extended a form for her to sign. She read the typewritten statement which stated that the undersigned had been permitted to take her personal prayer book into the USSR, providing she also took it back when she left.

Before the traveller boarded the outbound bus the customs officer asked a single additional question: "Why did you tell your aunt that we had confiscated the prayer book?"

Another familiar aspect of Soviet life was everywhere evident as I began my late-afternoon walk back to the hotel. Weary women on their way home after an eight-hour shift in office or factory were doing the family shopping, standing in queues of varying lengths. According to Soviet statistics, something over half the households have refrigerators, though the ones we saw were very small. Food shopping, generally in a few different stores, is thus a daily chore. Tiredness, an understandable desire to get done and get home, and concern lest better quality goods be bought up before one gets to the head of a queue, combine to create a certain touchiness. Given the proverbial last straw, conflicts can sometimes break out.

Perhaps this was the reason for the incident in the lobby of a department store just around the corner from our hotel. The queue had turned into a shouting, gesticulating crowd encircling a man and a woman engaged in a serious fist fight. Between blows, each angrily accused the other of having stolen a place in the queue. The onlookers were divided about equally in their support for the combatants. Fortunately, a nearby policeman soon appeared, since some of those in opposing cheering sections had begun to eye one another warily. In response to the officer's barked order to settle down, the belligerents were separated and the shouting stopped.

"Now," said the policeman, taking out a notebook and pencil, "tell me what started all this."

Immediately in an unharmonious duet, the two fighters blurted out their versions. They were joined within seconds by a shouted choral accompaniment from their respective camps.

Stunned by all that I had witnessed in the space of two or three minutes, I returned gratefully to the peace and quiet of our comfortable hotel room. A motherly-looking desk clerk, with a most musical Ukrainian accent, provided the boiling water for our instant coffee. By now we were almost addicted to the wonderful dark rye bread which I had purchased, along with some rather tasty Ukrainian sausage, just before I came upon the unscheduled boxing match. But the delicious birthday-party pastries given to us by our Christian friends were, in more than one sense, from another world.

17: *"Let us go into the house of the Lord."*

"Today I'll take you to the Darnetskaia church for the morning service," Petro told us as we got into the car. Driving toward the bridge over the mighty Dnieper river, he explained that Anna was not feeling too well this morning, or she would have come along. She would join us later that afternoon at their daughter Olena's place for a little lunch. We could then go to their own Sviatoshinskaia church for the evening service.

Knowing that Anna had a chronic heart problem, we asked how her general health had been. A sad look crossed Petro's usually smiling face.

"Well," he said, "she has better and worse days, but she keeps going regardless. You know," he continued, "our government seems to reserve scarce medicines for the élite or for show export. Even with my privileged veteran's status, I have not been able to get the medicine which would at least control her condition."

We had been with Petro for several days and would have frequent contacts with him during the next two weeks. In that time, we would be confronted with various frustrations inherent in the Soviet system. Despite all this, we would never again hear the tone of voice he used as he spoke of Anna's medical problem.

"See that break in the bridge railing over there?" Petro asked as we crossed over to the east bank of the Dnieper. "A bus driver who had been having serious marital problems drove his empty bus over the edge last night."

I mentioned the suicide at the hotel. "Yes," he sighed, "another Soviet citizen who could find no answers in his world to the tumultuous questions of life."

We knew that the Soviet media did not generally mention such things as suicides or airplane crashes. Frantic parents, for example, had waited at airports for days before finding out about disasters. How had Petro learned about the bus driver?

"Oh, that sort of thing spreads very quickly by word of mouth. Or else," he laughed, "we hear about it on the BBC!"

We had arrived at the church, a very attractive, new-looking building with an incredible amount of window space. It had been designed by Pastor Kunets, a pleasant forty-year-old to whom Petro immediately introduced us. Presumably Petro's skills as a repairman were known here as well, for he was asked to check on the malfunctioning of the loudspeaker system. Lil and I were taken on a quick tour of the church, ending up in the basement office.

"So you liked our building – except for the toilets, perhaps?" the pastor asked as we settled into our chairs. "Fortunately, because of some American visitors and the support of a Soviet government official we will soon be changing that unpleasant situation."

The Americans, part of an official delegation, were accompanied on a recent tour of the building by a Soviet official. Anxious to prove that Baptists in the USSR are not persecuted, but are given every necessary freedom, the official had asked what they thought of the building. The plumbing-conscious Americans had replied that the building was fine, but the primitive, pungent toilets were terrible.

Shortly afterwards the same official had visited the pastor, demanding to know why the toilets were not as modern as the rest of the building. Were the Baptists deliberately trying to make the Soviet government look bad in the eyes of American visitors? The pastor's mild rejoinder that the nearest sewer line was about half a kilometer away was answered by a sputter, "Well, well . . . we'll just have to work something out together. This simply cannot remain as it is now." He chuckled as he finished the story.

Among the brethren who would be speaking that morning was a visitor from our ancestral village of Borodianka. We introduced ourselves, adding that my grandfather had been one of the founders of the church there and that we were planning to visit the village during the next weekend. His warm assurance that this would make us doubly welcome increased our already eager anticipation. Clearly, both rural and urban Baptist churches were doing well in the Ukraine, location of about 40% of the denomination's membership.

The pastor's voice broke into our conversation. "Next time, dear brother, you will preach for us. Today you will, of course bring greetings. And," he added with a smile, "please feel free to bring a few greetings from Mark, John, or Paul to our church."

I was somewhat surprised that this Union church should be so different in this respect from those which we had visited in Leningrad and Moscow. As we moved up the stairs I asked the pastor if my participation would create any difficulties for him. I was not part of an official delegation and Soviet authorities had been pressuring church leaders to curb participation by foreign visitors.

"I don't know what they do up north," he responded. "But here" he added, "I go by this Book."

The service format was familiar, but the impact was fresh and powerful. The choir in this and the central Iamskaia church, visited earlier in the week, proved that Ukrainian Baptist singers could more than hold their own with their Russian brethren. Unfortunately, our tape recorder batteries were running low and thus we got poor reproduction on the last two of four numbers.

The dedication ceremony was also familiar, much like those we had witnessed in many Canadian churches. The earnest young couple knelt, each of them offering a simple prayer. Holding the baby, the pastor gave a stirring prayer of dedication while the familiar sound of reverent whispering welled up from the standing congregation. As we thought of the intense social and political opposition which Christian parents in the USSR had to face, there was a new depth of meaning to the united promise to raise this child in the nurture and admonition of the Lord.

The congregation of about 350 worshippers was as open as the pastor, with dozens of them coming up to talk to us after the service. As usual, a number of them asked about favorite radio preachers, Canadian relatives that we might know, and why letters were not getting through. Petro waited patiently for us, exchanging greetings with old friends.

Pastor Kunets gave us his telephone number and we arranged to meet him later in the week. "Remember," he added as we left to go for lunch, "you'll be preaching at the mid-week service."

Scrupulously honest, the Ukrainian Baptists consistently use a very misleading expression. In the course of our visit we were regularly invited out for what was described as *mal'enki uzhen'* (literally, a little supper). Arriving at Olena's apartment that afternoon we discovered that the daughter was at least as guilty in the matter of word usage as the mother had been. The large table was completely covered with all kinds of food. What would not fit on the table was waiting in the kitchen. Fortunately, a few relatives had also been invited, or there would have been more point to Olena's good-natured protest after an hour or so that we had not really eaten anything.

The visitors, in their late sixties, made their own contribution to the conversational mix. They recalled the terrible thirties and the Stalin-created famine which took millions of Ukrainian lives. During the Second World War near-starvation conditions in German-occupied Kiev had prompted them to move out to the village. There at least, so they hoped, they would be able to find more food. As the German armies retreated, however, that same village was occupied and they had to endure another year of near starvation.

Familiar, but somehow meaningless statistics from my historical studies passed through my mind. There had probably been twenty million lives sacrificed in Stalin's collectivization of agriculture and five-year plans of crash industrialization. Another twenty million Soviet citizens had died as a result of World War II. The mind cannot seem to grasp the enormity of the suffering represented by these figures. It needs the concrete and the individual.

"There was not even a single crust of bread to give to my pleading child. I walked miles through the streets of Kiev, looking for any kind of food. Everywhere there were corpses, some lying on the ground, some frozen in a seated position. Our main street, Kreshchatik, looks beautiful now, but I remember when it was a sea of flame, for block after block. You've seen the memorial at Babi Yar, with its stark figures toppling into the ravine? The execution of thousands of Jews and their bulldozer-burial was terrible. They say that the ground heaved for days afterwards, as the not-yet-dead struggled to get out of the mass grave. But the Jews of Kiev were not the only ones who suffered – there was probably not a single family among our one million inhabitants who did not lose someone."

Two expressions which we had heard often before in Leningrad and Moscow were repeated a number of times that afternoon. "At least we have enough to eat now" and "Pray God that there will not be another war." Was it time, place, repetition or roots which gave those familiar expressions their unfamiliar, crushing impact that afternoon in Kiev?

Little Sasha, Olena and Victor's chubby four year-old son had long ago fallen asleep in his doting grandmother's arms. He awoke smiling sleepily, being caressed with a chorus of questions about an earlier tummy-ache. "I think it is getting better now, thank you," he replied, with an almost comical childish gravity.

"Given the Soviet people's overwhelming opposition to war," Lil observed, "it seems strange to find so many war toys in the department stores. I wonder who is buying them?"

There was an embarrassed silence. A slightly guilty look at a sample of such toys in a corner of the apartment was followed by some stammered grandparental explanations. "But it is impossible to deny pleading children when they . . ."

"How do you like our stores?", asked Olena's husband, a gracious, but rather quiet interior decorator. "I do up the show windows in a number of department stores in Kiev," Viktor continued. "Do you have that kind of thing in Canada?"

We expressed our admiration for some of the attractive displays which we had seen, but did not make the obvious comparison between their somewhat outdated, small-town quality and the current Western equivalent. Petro smiled appreciatively and observed that he had been trying to tell his family about shopping facilities in Canada as he had seen them. A Soviet observer, seeing the superabundance of goods available there, Petro laughingly suggested, might well conclude that Canada had already attained the promised goal of communism: "From each according to his ability, to each according to his needs."

"And how is my sister Sonya getting along?", asked one of the visitors. "Is her husband still a preacher?"

We informed her that both Sonya and her husband were in poor health. She had been suffering from an increasingly crippling nerve disease for twenty-five years. Interestingly enough, we had talked to Sonya's retired preacher-husband shortly before our visit to the USSR. He had been wondering if his many letters to them had been getting through, since he had never received a reply.

There was a fairly long silence as Anna looked meaningfully at her aunt and uncle, both unbelievers. Finally the aunt replied, "We got all the letters, but we did not answer them. Both of us have fairly good jobs, and so do our children. You never know," she continued haltingly, "just what the authorities might do if we began corresponding with someone in the West. We could lose much, very much. If you see my sister and brother-in-law again, tell them that we are in good health and getting along well. But we can't write to him and it would even be better if he did not write to us any more."

It was time to get ready for the evening service. Petro would drive us over; Olena and her husband would take the bus. Anna, still not feeling very well, would remain with her grandson, who seemed delighted with the promise of playing a game, singing together — and a story before bedtime.

The church building was an old structure, the pastor somewhat correct in his response as we were introduced. Would I bring greetings? A couple of younger men protested. I should preach, they suggested. The pastor explained patiently that only members of official delegations could be asked to preach. One of the young men continued to argue that as an exchange scholar I was a guest of the Soviet government. In that sense, I could be considered part of an official delegation. The pastor held firm, going the rounds of the brethren assembled in the office – five minutes prior to the service – deciding who would preach that evening.

Again, the service followed the familiar pattern. The choir was excellent, and we looked regretfully at our dead tape recorder. Perhaps Petro could find the proper batteries somewhere. There had been none available in several department stores which we had checked earlier.

Seated next to us was a very large man, one of the brethren who had been asked to preach but had persistently refused. Since coming to the USSR I had enjoyed the unusual experience of being able to join congregational singing with as much volume as I cared to produce, and to take the preferred bass line, rather than the melody. My usually prominent voice was but one of many in Russian/Ukrainian Baptist congregations that evening. The metallically-resonant basso profundo voice of our seatmate made me sound like a timid tenor.

The service was over and the pastor was making some final routine announcements. Suddenly, a tall, dark-haired thirty-ish man came running up the aisle toward the pulpit. Throwing himself face down on the floor he began to cry out to God to forgive him and save his sinful soul, declaring that God Himself must have brought him into the service, for he had had no intention of coming. Great, shuddering sobs wracked his six-foot frame as he continued to bewail his wretchedly-sinful life and cry to God for mercy.

Members of the congregation prayed in urgent whispers while the startled pastor, gripping the edges of the pulpit, offered a few words and phrases of Christian counsel. A few moments later, a spontaneous chorus of praise to God accompanied the slow arising of a seemingly-transformed man. We had often seen people in evangelistic services at home respond to an altar call. We had never seen such a dramatic response to a pastor's reading of announcements.

As we stood around visiting after the service, a pleasant-looking young man came up to us and identified himself as being in charge of the young people's meeting which was about to start. Because I was both a pastor and a professor, it would be especially appropriate for the college-aged participants to have me attend and speak briefly. Carried away by the excitement of the last few minutes and eager to see these much-discussed young people in action, I did not even think to ask the pastor whether my participation would be permissible.

Most of the young people had already been present for the regular two-hour evening service, as had that evening's startling respondent, who gave a brief account of his wanderings throughout the USSR. Vibrant congregational singing, small group vocal and instrumental numbers, and passionate recitals of Christian poetry indicated that these young people really enjoyed their Christianity.

That they also took their Christianity very seriously was evident from the very beginning. After the first congregational hymn, the young man leading the service looked around at the group of about fifty and announced that there were some visitors present.

"We welcome you, friends," he said warmly. "Could you please tell us your names?"

One of three rather hard-looking young men stood up and announced in a mocking tone that his mother had named him Mikhail. In response to the leader's next question as to whether he was a believer or an unbeliever,

Mikhail snorted contemptuously, "An unbeliever, of course!" His two friends nodded in agreement.

"Then we are very sorry for you," came a chorus of earnest voices from the church young people.

The service continued for about two hours. The three unbelievers kept peppering me and the young people with pretty well every kind of rationalist-scientific objection to Christian belief that I had encountered from skeptical college students and professors in Canada. Initially frustrated by my dreadfully inadequate Russian language, I was soon able to relax. The Christian young people, aided by one of the preaching brethren who had stayed for the service, handled the critics most admirably.

As we chatted after the service, I made a special point of going up to Mikhail, assuring him that I had appreciated his forthrightness and encouraging him to keep an open mind on these matters. "Yes," he responded, in a not-unfriendly tone, "it's good to discuss these questions, as well as political and scientific ones."

We left the church reluctantly, returning to our hotel almost fifteen hours after we had left that morning. A few days later we heard that the three atheists had continued their discussion with the young people for three hours after we left. They returned for another three-hour discussion with the young people's leaders a day later.

18: *The Professor, the Pastor and Some Other People*

Surprisingly enough, the promised visa for a visit to our home village was ready on the day promised. Half-expecting a recurrence of my on-again-off-again interview with the Soviet academic in Moscow, I asked the Academy of Sciences officer if my scheduled meeting with Professor Baranov at the university was still on.

"I can't see why not, since it has already been arranged," he replied in a puzzled tone. "I'll phone and check, if you wish." A quick call confirmed the time and place.

Wanting to check a few items in the card catalogue before meeting with Professor Baranov for a few minutes' discussion on sources, I hurried off to the university. Strawberry season was still on, with prices going down at the stalls as more berries came on the market. I stopped briefly at a nearby stall, its exceptionally long queue testifying to something especially desirable – plump, luscious-looking cherries, in this case.

Professor Baranov of the Department of History, was accompanied by a colleague from the law faculty. We exchanged pleasantries and I asked Baranov about any special collections or individual sources on pre-Revolutionary Russian Baptist history. There seemed to be nothing that he could add to the list of those sources with which I was already acquainted. His interest was in the more recent past, mine in origins and growth of the Russian Baptist movement.

"And what is your general thesis?", he asked just before I got ready to return to the university library.

Adequate for general conversation, my Russian was not really good enough for treatment of sophisticated historical and philosophical questions. Haltingly, I explained that I considered Baptism to be an essentially religious movement, distinguished from others in Russia's past by its Biblicism, belief in justification by faith, and the believers' church. It had arisen partly in response to deteriorated conditions in Orthodoxy and the older Russian sects and partly because of outside religious influences during the period 1855-75. Admittedly, socio-economic and political factors during this period had affected the emergence of Baptism and had had some influence on its course of development. These non-religious factors were not central, however, and the Baptists' views on all questions were primarily a reflection of their basic religious convictions.

"Very difficult to accept such a thesis," Baranov announced, when I had finished.

He then proceeded to offer the standard Marxist interpretation. Baptism was, of course, really a social phenomenon, representing but one facet of Russia's capitalist development in the nineteenth century. Its leadership was bourgeois and its mass membership was drawn from the poor peasantry and a very few, backward members of the working class. With developing class consciousness, the religious façade would be exposed, showing that the *real* influences and interests of all those involved were, all along, socio-economic.

The anticipated few minutes' questioning about sources turned into a free-wheeling two-hour discussion. We talked about the basic nature of reality, social causation and individual perception, the theory and practice of Soviet educational and religious policies. As the debate proceeded, I was scarcely aware of my surprisingly increased fluency in Russian. On the other hand, both of us were undoubtedly aware of the steadily-increasing heat with which we expressed our opinions.

A rather strange byway in our discussion involved President Carter's Baptist affiliation. Looking earnestly at me, and with an almost pathetic note in his voice, Baranov declared: "You've seen our Baptists in the USSR. There are thousands, even hundreds of thousands of them. How many Baptists are there in China, I ask you? Yet Carter is becoming increasingly friendly towards the People's Republic of China. How can he do that? Logically, he should be improving relations with our country."

Perhaps rather unwisely, I resisted the temptation to comment on certain contradictions. How, for example, could one who had but recently insisted that religion was not a 'real' factor now turn around and argue that Carter's personal religious views should determine American foreign policy? We thus parted with reasonable friendliness.

The law professor gathered up his sheaf of notes of our conversation, presumably to corroborate those taken by Professor Baranov. I made my way back to the library slowly, remembering a single sentence spoken by the law professor when Baranov had left us alone for a few minutes to take a phone call.

"You know, Professor Nesdoly, it is hard, very hard for one in a position of authority to act according to Christian principles," he observed, rather sadly.

The fruit sellers were all gone as I walked back to the hotel, but Lil met me with a small bagful of cherries and an interesting account of how she had acquired them. The day was hot, the queue very long and the baby held by a weary mother very fretful. Solicitously, Lil had suggested to the others in the queue that the mother with the baby should be allowed to go immediately to the head of the line. This was greeted by loud refusals from all, without exception. They observed derisively that once that was granted they could all go home, bring their babies, and get this advantage over other citizens.

After about an hour of standing in line, Lil had moved up to the second position. The woman in front of her had bought a couple of kilos from the bottom of a case and had already paid for them. As she turned to go, noticing a few rotten cherries in her bag, she removed them and placed them neatly in a pile on the rough plank counter. The fruit seller was enraged.

"I sell you cherries at a good price and pack them nicely into your bag and you still throw them away," she screamed. Swiftly gathering up the offending handful of rotten cherries she threw them straight into the startled customer's face.

I shared my day's experiences with Lil as we travelled along to meet Pastor Kunets at the designated meeting place on the east side of the city. Kiev's subway system, less extensive than those of Moscow and Leningrad, was similarly rapid, and within a few minutes we were chatting with the pastor as we walked over toward a nearby taxi stand.

Two women were ahead of us: a young mother holding an infant, and a vigorous-looking woman about sixty years of age, burdened down with two large shopping bags. The arrival of a taxi created a certain problem of precedence. Should the elder woman or the baby-carrier be allowed to go first?

The young mother was of the same opinion Lil had expressed in the cherry-buying queue. The older woman would have voted with the majority on that occasion. Both lunged for the taxi's open door.

Showing commendable speed and agility, the old

woman threw a very nice hip-check at the critical moment. Then, scarcely losing any momentum and still clutching the shopping bags, the sprightly sexagenarian leaped into the front seat. Her triumph was not complete, however, for she still had one muscular leg outside the taxi.

Down, but not out, the resourceful young mother — holding her baby with one arm — grabbed the taxi door and slammed it shut. More precisely, the door would have slammed shut — if the old woman's leg had not been in the way.

We waited for a few minutes as the rather shaken young woman eventually got her taxi. Embarrassed, Pastor Kunets assured us that "it does not always happen this way."

As we drove along toward the church, the pastor carried on a casual conversation with the taxi driver, asking him about his background and outside interests. On arrival at the church, Kunets insisted on paying the cabdriver, giving him an extra ruble and suggesting pleasantly that he might like to visit the church himself sometime. Muttering his thanks, the cabby drove off and we walked into the church yard.

"Poor man," the pastor sighed, "who will show him love, if not the Christians? You saw those two women at the taxi stand. Life can be very hard in our country, and frustration and bitterness sometimes breaks out into open conflict."

We were reminded of an observation made by a number of believers who told us sadly, "Yes, ours is officially a godless country, and since God is love, sooner or later a godless country becomes a loveless country."

We were pleasantly surprised at the turnout of around one hundred and fifty people. Even more remarkable was the fact that a couple of benches at the back of the church were filled with unbelievers.

"They came because our people invite them or because they've been attracted by the choral or orchestral music," Pastor Kunets explained. "Every week some of them remain after the service to speak to me about spiritual matters. In fact," he concluded, "many who are now members came in this way."

Among the members present that evening was a delightful midget, standing about three feet six inches short. Adored by everyone for his unfailingly sunny disposition, he presented an especially endearing sight when he took his place in the church orchestra. He played the baritone horn.

"See that young man in the second row on the right?" Pastor Kunets asked as we sat together on the platform. "He came to Kiev from Moscow a while ago and has been living at a hotel since then. Though apparently not working at any specific job, he always seems to have plenty of money. It's very peculiar."

The story continued after the service. "That young man first came to a service here a few weeks back and asked to see me afterwards. He expressed a desire to join the church. When I asked him why, he seemed to be struck speechless, but finally blurted out: 'Why? So that we can fight these communists together!' I informed him that he must have made some mistake when he came here, since we were not concerned with fighting communists, but with preaching the gospel of Jesus Christ, and instructing Christians in Biblical truth. That very same day," Pastor Kunets concluded, "I was informed that he had gone to the Reform Baptist church and apparently managed to convince them that he was truly a repentant sinner, since they took him in."

We arrived at the pastor's apartment, which was considerably larger than most because of his family of nine children. One of these, a chubby ten-year-old boy, had muscular dystrophy. Though already unable to walk, he seemed to be extraordinarily cheerful as he joked with his brothers and pulled himself across the floor with muscular arms. Early symptoms of the disease had appeared in one or possibly two of the younger children.

Mrs. Kunets, but recently home from the hospital after the birth of her ninth child, had prepared another one of those celebrated "little suppers." In the middle of the crowded table stood a huge container of freshly-made strawberry juice, while an already-poured tankard, holding about a litre or so of the juice, stood at each place setting. Our protests that this would be much too much were met with a puzzled look and assurance that the pastor and his teen-aged son drank a couple of these per meal. Embarrassingly enough, the drawn-out meal and delightful conversation did eventually include a somewhat sheepish request for "perhaps just a partial refill."

Pastor Kunets had been trying to negotiate the purchase of a car, or preferably a van, to accommodate his large family. "Of course," he added, "a van would also be very useful for transporting church members and instruments when we visit another church for special services. But just recently a Soviet official told me bluntly that the régime was not about to start providing vans for churches, adding that, as a preacher I would be unlikely to get any kind of car at all. My protests about constitutional guarantees of non-discrimination on religious grounds were met with mocking laughter. Oh well," he chuckled, "sooner or later we'll get some kind of car, which we'll be able to trade somewhere for a van."

Looking through a photo album, I noticed a familiar-looking face. He was about thirty, much-travelled in the West, and one of the prominent preaching brethren in another Union church. "Yes, I know him quite well too," said Pastor Kunets with a rather grim smile. "He's all eyes, all ears – and all mouth too."

I recalled an incident from my 1971 visit to a Russian evangelical church in Helsinki. The pastor, a former citizen of the USSR, had received word that an official delegation of five Baptists from the USSR would be visiting Helsinki. "Five," he repeated thoughtfully, "– that means four brethren and one spy." Sharing this observation with an Independent Russian Baptist preacher on this trip, I asked whether he would agree with the assessment.

"No," he replied with a little laugh, "because there has to be someone to spy on the spy!"

It was past midnight and raining furiously. Fortunately, Pastor Kunets was able to get a taxi in which we sputtered our way through occasionally axle-high torrents on the five-mile ride back to the hotel. The initially rather frightened desk clerk smiled in evident relief, greeting us pleasantly as we stood for a moment in the lobby. Entering the elevator we heard her only-half-humorous parting suggestion: "If you keep coming in so late every night, I'll have to send the police out to search for you!"

19: *Kiev Kaleidoscope*

Old and new, familiar and foreign blend together during our quickly-passing days in Kiev. The starkly-simple modernity of the concert hall provides a technically-superb setting for sophisticated young Ukrainians in antique peasant costumes, performing centuries-old traditional folk songs and dances. Cars screech around the equestrian statue of the seventeenth-century Cossack hero, Bohdan Khmelnitsky, while jet trails span the skies above the thousand-year-old Golden Gates of Kiev. At one of Orthodoxy's most sacred places, the *Pecherskaia Lavra* (Monastery of the Caves) a much decorated Honored Artist of the USSR has a display of micro-sculptures, done under an electron microscope. The prize item is a gold padlock with seven moving parts. It is one fifty-thousandth the size of a poppy seed. Passing through the monastery's caves and encountering yet another display-case full of saints' bones, an irreverent Western tourist breaks into a rousing chorus of "Dem bones, dem bones, dem dry bones!"

The Soviet attempt to reproduce corn flakes needs some additional work on both taste and texture. Walking down Kreshchatik one day we see a sign: *Varenichna*. Mouths watering at the memory of both mothers' mass production of these delicate filled dumplings, Lil and I order two batches. One bite convinces us that these are not in the least like our mothers used to make. We move quickly across the street to the free market to buy some fruit.

Here, directly across from a large bust of Lenin, founder of Soviet Russia's state socialism, peasants conduct a bustling free-enterprise sale of goods from their private plots.

Twentieth-century transportation is much appreciated as a friend offers to drive us to a medieval church to view some celebrated icons. He decides to take a short cut, becoming almost panicky as he discovers that the road is closed. "What they wouldn't do to me for bringing foreigners through here!" he mutters, wheeling the car around in a screeching U-turn. The twentieth-century Soviet psychiatric hospital we have just left has about it the appearance of a Dickensian insane asylum.

Presumably, after six weeks in the USSR, our Russian language is improving. Speaking with some grandmothers and their grandchildren in a park one morning, Lil explains after a few minutes that she must leave to catch the opening of the foreign-currency store. They look at her sympathetically and inform her that the manager will not let her in there – "That store is only for foreigners, dearie!" one of them sighs. A recurring leg cramp grips Lil at around three a.m. Awakened by her groans my first word is *Chto*? (What is it?)

A member of the Darnetskaia church is insistent that we visit him and his wife, holding out the additional incentive of strawberries fresh from the village and a magnificent view of Kiev from his eleventh-floor apartment. Half-reluctantly we agree, cancelling a previous appointment with Petro and Anna. Home contacts with new friends will provide an additional dimension to our impressions of Christians' lives in the USSR.

The grey Soviet-style apartment building is easily found, being directly across the street from the Kiev Opera House, a large Victorian structure with a striking pink and white stucco exterior. Fortunately, the elevator is merely slow, rather than *Na remont*. (Under repair, and thus not operating.)

A puzzled-looking teenager opens the door, looking no less puzzled after we inform her that we are the Christians from Canada. Her mother is at work and her father, as planned, left for the village that very afternoon. "Presumably to pick more of those strawberries he promised us," I mutter to Lil as we return to the elevator after we have taken a quick look at Kiev from the balcony of our insistent friend's apartment. (Petro tells us later that there is an old Ukrainian saying: "Come and visit us when we are not at home.") Lil suggests that we make the most of a spoiled evening by catching the second half of the year-end concert at the opera house.

Petro drops us off about a block from the Reform Baptist church, now registered and meeting unmolested in a large, newly-constructed building. We are introduced to the pastor, an attractive, man in his late thirties. Somewhat surprisingly, he also holds a teaching position in one of the state schools. I am asked to preach but, for the first time anywhere in the USSR, I am also asked what I plan to say.

At the end of the service, a plump, grey-haired woman comes up to the platform, introducing herself as the wife of a well-known Baptist dissident preacher. I ask her if she knows of a certain Christian researcher in the West who has publicized her husband's cause. She answers evasively. Afterwards, safely out in the street, she is very open, asking us to pass on greetings to the said researcher, a close personal friend. But to admit in the USSR that one knows him is a sure ticket to prison. Had we noticed the teenager who had listened so attentively as we were speaking to one another in English? She speaks very good English and has just joined the church. No one is quite sure yet whether this new member is a sister or a spy.

"It is puzzling," our new acquaintance informs us, "that the present pastor and my husband were charged with the same crimes at the same time. Yet my husband is now in prison. Were it not for the kindness of friends and relatives, I don't know how I and the children would survive. In the five years that my husband has been in prison, the present pastor has not once even asked me how I am getting along."

Not wishing to leave everything to the last, busy week, I ask Lil to take our Kiev-Leningrad railway tickets to the appropriate bureau for verification. She agrees readily, since she will be sightseeing in that area anyway. Booking tickets could be time-consuming, but simple verification would take but a few minutes.

She waits in line from 10 a.m. to noon, not a little distressed by the shouting and weeping going on in front of her. Soviet travellers are informed that the seats which they had booked in good faith are not available. Others discover that the very trains on which they expected to travel do not even exist. Questions and complaints are met with stony silence or rough orders to get out of the way in order that the next person can be served.

Lil gets to the head of the line at one minute to twelve, but the clerk slams the shutter down, announcing that there will be a one-hour lunch break. With increasing impatience Lil waits as the Soviet queue artists flow around in front of her. At three o'clock she is back to the window. An angry clerk scolds her for not having the hotel do this for her, ignoring Lil's explanation that we are not tourists, and thus have to do this ourselves. Most unwillingly, the clerk checks the records, bangs the stamp down twice on the offending tickets and throws them across the counter.

Total time required for confirmation: approximately

fifteen seconds. Total waiting time: approximately four hours.

A familiar voice calls my name in the hotel lobby. It belongs to the mother of my closest friend from teenage years. We exchange warm greetings as she informs me that she will be visiting her ancestral village, even as we will. We arrange to take her to the service at the Iamskaia church, getting thoroughly lost and riding the bus – at no extra charge – for an extra hour. We arrive at the church to find it being ripped up and renovated. Unfamiliar-looking brethren at this Baptist church assure us that they began the work last Sunday morning. I remember eventually that the Baptists share this meeting place with a Seventh-day Adventist congregation.

My friend's mother reminds us of her concern for her youngest son, the only one of three boys who is not a believer. He is also visiting the USSR, taking a holiday from his engineering job in Nairobi. The next morning we meet for breakfast, exchanging boyhood stories. We interject a few words of witness to which he is unresponsive. Hearing that he is at least very much interested in music, we invite him to join us for Sunday evening's service in Leningrad two weeks hence. He seems interested enough to ask for the address of the church.

As we walk along the road from the Darnetskaia church, Pastor Kunets gives a humorous account, complete with pantomime illustration, of how a recent American visitor kept looking over his shoulder for potential muggers. We laugh together. A couple of days later Lil is all alone in a very old section of Kiev. Her artistic eye spots a particularly striking view of some old buildings and she adjusts her camera for the perfect shot. Suddenly, she is struggling to retain possession of that camera which an angry man is trying to take away from her. Her shouts for help bring none, but her assailant, not prepared to risk getting caught, releases her and disappears.

Shaken, but relieved that it was not even worse, she heads out into a more open street. Her assailant reappears and the whole scene is re-enacted. It takes both of us a long time to settle down on that night before our long-awaited trip to the village.

20: *Going Home*

"So you are going out to the village," the smiling clerk observed as we shared our excitement with her. "You have a visa, of course?" she asked nervously. I answered that of course we did. "Please forgive me," she continued, "but if it's not too much trouble . . . I personally wouldn't ask . . . But I have to see the actual visa. You understand."

Assuring her that I did indeed understand, I extended our passports, opened to the section containing the visas. "Yes, yes – everything in order," she announced with a relieved smile, returning the extended documents even before I had time to withdraw my hand.

Petro was waiting at the curb. Our suggestion that we should fill the gas tank was met with the reply that he had already done so. Previous attempts to buy gas on our extended travels throughout Kiev had been equally unsuccessful. "My car doesn't really take any gas," he had declared nonchalantly, speeding up as we approached the rarely-seen filling stations.

Fortunately, neither Petro nor his son had been at the counter in the foreign currency store when we had bought some items for them. Their later questions about the price paid were answered by our perfectly true, if not strictly relevant, reports that neither of us was especially good at mathematics.

"Anna packed a little lunch for us," said Petro as we left the suburbs. "There's a pine forest along the way where we can stop and have a bite – maybe even find some wild strawberries."

Scattered, tiny, but incredibly flavourful, the strawberries were delicious. They were just as wonderful as those we had picked during our childhoods in Saskatchewan – on land homesteaded by people from the village of Borodianka.

"You'll be able to see the village in a minute," said Petro as we drove out of the forest and through the more familiar open plains.

We were prepared for the traditional long main street of the typical Ukrainian village, but the towering smoke-stack of the huge tractor factory seemed out of place in this peaceful rural setting. Modern apartment blocks and individual bungalows contrasted sharply with ancient clay-plastered whitewashed cottages. Yet even the thatch-roofed cottages could not escape modernity. Here and there, the highly-prized crane's nest perched alongside a television antenna.

We entered the village near the railway station, travelling along the main street, named after Lenin, of course. Quickly finding my second cousin's home, we had the most peculiar sense of *déja vu*. The gate, the layout of the flower beds and especially the hilled rows of vegetables in the garden were just as we had always known them. The impression of familiarity became even stronger as we talked with Cousin Marta. Her rather colloquial Russo-Ukrainian dialect was exactly the same as that spoken by our recently-deceased grandparents, who had left Borodianka seventy years earlier.

She apologized for the condition of the house, which was in the midst of major renovation, but insisted that we should have a bit of lunch together anyway. It would just take her a minute to heat things up, during which time we should go out into the strawberry patch and enjoy this year's very good crop. Protests that we had just had lunch en route to the village were brushed aside as irrelevant. We complied, observing that she was just as persuasive as her son had been when we had such a pleasant visit with him and his wife a few days previously.

We sat down at the table. Knowing her to be an unbeliever, I took advantage of my visitor status and asked Petro to say grace. Briefly, simply, but with great power, he thanked God for the gift of His Son, Jesus Christ, and for salvation through His blood. Catching his breath, he went on to ask God's blessing on the food and prayed that He would reveal Himself to this home, which had extended such gracious hospitality to us. Cousin Marta, obviously deeply stirred, could only whisper, "Thank you for those wonderful words."

Impatient relatives from Lil's half of our family background were soon at the door. Petro returned to Kiev and we walked the short block or so to great uncle Evtukh's house. Three brothers had migrated to Canada, including Lil's maternal grandfather. Evtukh and another brother, now deceased, had remained. Here, the situation was what one might have expected: the Canadians were believers; the two who remained were not. And yet, in the case of one Ukrainian-Canadian's family, it was not the Canadians but rather those who remained in the south-western part of the USSR, who were Christians. In fact, an uncle was the respected manager of a collective farm, making free use of the farm trucks to bring people to church services.

We asked about the local church, surprised to hear the Baptists still referred to as 'Stundists.' (*Stunde*, from the German for *hour*, in reference to informal hours of prayer and Bible study) Originally, over one hundred years ago, the term was used mockingly by Orthodox believers to refer to fellow-villagers who had become converts to evangelical Christianity, as preached in nearby German colonies. Some relatives knew the location of the Sunday services but no one knew their precise time. One of them would find out for us "if we really insisted on going."

The Ukrainian's commitment to provide the very best food available for his honored guest was abundantly demonstrated at great uncle Evtukh's; at his next-door daughter's place; and also at the Buzovetskii's, relatives of both Lil and myself. We met Hanya, a sad-looking divorcee, who had been scheduled to visit us in Canada a couple of years earlier. Pressed to explain why she had not come, after permission had been granted and the ticket provided, she looked at us meaningfully and answered, "Please – don't ask."

Unfortunately, these particular Ukrainians also believed that honored guests should be hosted with an abundance of liquors of various kinds. Puzzled at our refusal to join in this part of the celebration, they did not feel constrained to limit their own intake. In fact, a few suggested that they would be glad to drink not only their own share, but ours as well. Initially, the requested children's stories and folk songs were enjoyable. As the evening wore on, however, we noticed that various singers attempted to make up for decreasing quality by increasing volume.

Excitement, the scarcely-avoidable overeating, an unfamiliar bed in a rarely-used and somewhat musty room – all combined to produce an almost sleepless night. On the other hand, both of us managed to get quite a bit of unexpected exercise. Several times on that pitch-black night we walked through the back yard, carefully shielding our sputtering matches and trying to avoid running into the rabbit cages. The latch on the garden gate gave us a bit of trouble at first, but was more easily handled on second and subsequent trips. A short walk down a curving, slightly uneven path, and we had arrived at the 'facilities,' equipped with a recent copy of *Pravda*.

Early Sunday morning, a neighbor arrived to escort us to church. On hearing that I was the grandson of one of the founding members, Nestor Andreyevich, preacher of the gospel for over sixty years, her lined face broke into a beaming smile.

"He has served the Lord well," she declared, "and earned his eternal reward." Quietly, but with both fluency and fervor, she continued – clearly for the benefit of our unbelieving relatives – to present a testimony of her own faith in Christ and the basic gospel message.

Later that day, Lil gave her one of our carefully-hoarded New Testaments. Hugging this treasure and weeping tears of joy, she informed Lil that she had been longing for a new Bible, since the one she had was falling apart, missing several pages, and scarcely legible in places because of the faded print. Her only family consisted of an alcoholic son, for whom she was much burdened.

"Of course," she concluded, "it goes without saying that my Christian brothers and sisters are a real encouragement and support to me. And now I can go down among the strawberries every day and read this beautiful New Testament."

As we walked along the whitewashed, tin-roofed house that served as a church we noticed a gaunt, serious man, about sixty years old, coming along the street. As we were introduced he smiled warmly, if a bit weakly, having just returned from hospitalization for major surgery.

"So, you are the grandson of one of our pioneers – and a preacher as well as a professor! You will, of course, bring us a word this morning," he announced, rather than asked.

I introduced the pastor to a newly-discovered relative, the young aeronautical engineer at whose Kiev home we had recently enjoyed a very pleasant evening. "Delighted to meet you," the pastor responded. "I know your wife's grandfather quite well. He occasionally preaches at funerals here. Do come and visit our services whenever you are here in the village. Some people are reluctant to attend church, fearing the political and social consequences. But we must remember that we'll all have to answer before God some day. And what is man compared to Him?"

The frail, sickly man had been speaking with remarkable strength and urgency. Polite, but non-committal, his young listener had thanked him for the invitation and we continued on toward the church together.

"An aeronautical engineer, aren't you?", the pastor observed. "You should have been at the meetings in Kiev last month. American astronaut James Irwin was there. He spoke so marvellously about the wonders of God's universe and of his own faith in Christ."

Presumably this was not the first time that our charming engineer-relative had attended a Baptist service. During our visit to his Kiev apartment he had told us of a previous visit to a Baptist church. Himself of Orthodox background, though not a believer, he had been struck by the absence of internal decoration, holy relics, altars, sacred icons. "To what *do* the Baptists pray?" he asked in polite puzzlement.

Approximately seventy people had gathered for the morning service. The pastor spoke briefly, as did a visitor from a nearby village and a sturdy forty-year-old man who would be taking over pastoral duties in Borodianka. Women outnumbered men by about two to one and the average age was somewhat higher than it was in the urban churches we had visited. This little church also had a choir, consisting of about thirty-five hearty singers, who crowded together at the front of the room each time the pastor announced: *"Khor proslavit' Gospoda."* (The choir will praise God.)

We had been enjoying the service immensely, but then the pastor announced that Samoyil Ivanovich Nesdoly, grandson of one of the founding members of the church would bring a word. I was almost drowned in a tidal wave of emotion. Since entering the Ukraine we had experienced an increasing awareness of our ethnic roots, an impression much strengthened by our visit to this, our ancestral village. Similarly, as we attended services and met with fellow-Christians in Kiev, we had begun to understand and appreciate more fully our goodly spiritual heritage.

Perhaps it was the combined force of all this that suddenly bore down upon me so that I could not even speak. Here was a large, grandmotherly woman who had asked me earlier about her relatives in our home town in Saskatchewan, saddened to learn that they had no time for the gospel. Here was a vigorous man of eighty-two, boyhood chum of my father. He told me confidentially that on the collective farm bordering the village non-Christian workers felt that they had to steal, or else they would starve.

"Back in 1930," he whispered, "the authorities came out from Kiev and took everything – everything, down to the last piece of thread in our houses."

Everywhere, lined faces gave mute testimony of the decades of suffering and of triumphant spiritual strength. They had lived through three revolutions and a bloody First World War. Then from 1918-1920, there had been a tumultuous civil war, during which nearby Kiev changed hands fourteen times. A bare half-dozen years of respite had given way to the horrors of forced collectivization in 1930, ushering in the crash industrialization and Stalinist terror of the 1930s. Then came the titanic struggles of World War II, which had fertilized these peaceful fields with the blood and bones of multiplied thousands.

I recalled a Canadian friend's visit to his home village. A broken-spirited uncle had told of his final memories of the German occupation. "They made us dig a big pit. Then they lined up our children around the edge and shot them. At gun point, they forced us to shovel the earth on the children's still-quivering bodies."

And it was these same people, who had kept the faith and maintained the testimony of the church through all that, who assured me humbly that they were honored to have *me* in their midst. Somehow I stumbled through about twenty minutes of a simple gospel message. As I prepared to take my seat again, I was stopped by a chorus of protesting voices.

"No, no – you must tell us more. Tell us about the church which you are pastoring and of your work as a Christian professor."

And so I went on – somehow, the words came. Tear-stained yet beaming, faces offered mute encouragement. Heartfelt exclamations of *Slava Bogu*! (Glory to God!), periodically broke through my halting account of how a number of college students had come to faith in Christ.

A quick glance at my watch informed me that the service had been going on for two and one-half hours, and yet the people kept asking for more. The communion service which followed lifted us to even greater heights of spiritual exaltation. Here were the familiar large, home-baked loaf, single silver cup, and the heart-gripping minor strains of the traditional hymn, "Let us go to Golgotha, my brother." Neither before nor since, in dozens of communion services, have we felt anything quite like the depths of truth shared that afternoon, as we joined to "remember the Lord's death until He come."

The communal meal was a delightful continuation of fellowship and, along with the morning's experiences generally, probably much like first-century Christian practice. The surroundings were plainer and the place settings considerably less uniform, but in every other sense the large bustling peasant women who heaped the table with traditional Ukrainian dishes were full equals – and more – of their urban Christian sisters. Unfortunately, the previous day's feasting had not yet worn off; thus, despite the wonderful food and the insistence of our hostesses, we had to plead that, "the spirit is willing, but the flesh is weak."

The incoming pastor came up to the table following a brief consultation with some of the brethren. "This has been a wonderful day," he declared, "but it must not stop here. I am going to rent a car and we will take you around to several neighboring villages. People there will be most interested to hear you speak."

His enthusiasm was infectious and the prospect of sharing the gospel with other villagers extremely tempting. But we were expected to be back in our Kiev hotel before midnight and the visa specified that we had been granted permission to visit the village of Borodianka – by implication, no other villages. Reluctantly, both of us agreed that it was best to bow to the orders of the Soviet Caesar in this matter.

I remembered the experience of a Canadian-Ukrainian friend, who tended to be very impatient with official regulations – especially Soviet ones. He had been visiting the USSR and had overstayed his visa time period. Promptly summoned to the police station, he was sternly informed of the seriousness of this crime and its possible consequences. The officer then suggested that there was a way out. If the Canadian agreed to make periodic reports to Soviet authorities about Ukrainian-Canadian attitudes, the charges would be dropped.

As he told me the story, my friend stopped at that point. When I asked him about his reply to the officer's suggestion he drawled, "Well, I told him *I* wasn't interested, but I gave him *your* name!"

We finally left the church, four hours after we had arrived for the morning service. A profound sense of being one in the bonds of Christian faith had united us with the believers though we had known them for only these few hours. Perhaps we would come back one day. It was all but certain that none of them would be allowed to visit us in Canada. But for Christians, the traditional parting words *Do svedanye* (Until we meet again) are not limited to the hope of meeting again only in life or time. Though not enriched by the bonds of a common Christian faith, family ties had also been forged during our visit to the village. Two sturdy children chomped delightedly on their wonderful Canadian chewing gum. Cousin Nikolai, he of the haunted look and the headful of wartime nightmares, waved and walked on. The curly-haired architect stood next to his railway-worker brother, who was witty and gracious, but plagued by an apparently unconquerable drinking problem. The railway man's wife and mother came from the kitchen, wiping their hands on their aprons, kissing us tearful good-byes, and reminding us to pass on the warmest greetings to Lil's parents. Gentle old Uncle Evtukh gripped our hands fiercely, looked deeply into our eyes, then simply broke down. We stood with our arms around him for a few minutes, tears dropping on the hard-packed earth. Then the three of us walked off together to the bus stop.

"*Do svedanye?*", we whispered to one another.

Hanya, who was going to accompany us back to Kiev on the electric train, got on the bus a few stops later. "So you didn't take the samovar after all," she observed, settling down across from us.

We had been sorely tempted by the offer of this family heirloom, dating from the early nineteenth century. Probably worth around $3000, on the North American antique market, it was being stored in the chicken coop at Uncle Evtukh's place. Lil's parents had openly brought three other samovars out of the USSR with no customs problem on the occasion of their first trip to the village. But on their second, several years later, they had been refused permission to take out this particular samovar – a national treasure, apparently.

"No," we said, continuing our discussion as we got on the waiting electric train. "After Dad's experience, and the even worse problems of a Canadian visitor who was taking home some family gifts, we decided to leave the samovar. The only way we would agree to take it would be if we had an export certificate, and we don't know how to get one."

"But you should have told me before," Hanya declared. "I know someone who works in that department in Kiev and I'm sure I can get you the official paper. Give me the phone number of your hotel room and I'll get back to you early in the week. It will then be a simple matter for me to take the train out to Borodianka and get the samovar for you before you leave for Leningrad next Saturday."

We continued our conversation, making reference to the wonderful experience of joining for worship that morning in the little church just three blocks from her parents' home. Sensing her genuine interest, we continued to present the gospel message and the basic principles of the Christian life. Curious fellow-passengers kept their eyes fixed on us, listening intently.

"Yes, yes dear Samoyil Ivanovich," she interjected, "I can see that the Christians have a joy and peace that I do not know. But if I believed as you do, I would lose all I have: my Party position, my job as a chemical engineer, and the privileges which these two positions bring. I would lose all my friends, and life in the Soviet Union would be very hard for me – very hard," she concluded, with an anguished sigh.

We had one Russian New Testament left. She took it willingly, turning it over and over in her hands and whispering: "Thank you so very much. Thank you, thank you, thank you."

The train had entered one of the Kiev stations. Hanya insisted on accompanying us by subway to our hotel. She embraced us tightly as we parted, promising to get back to us in a day or two about the samovar.

We never heard from her again.

21: *Kiev Coda*

It seemed that I had exhausted the available resources of the University and Academy of Sciences libraries. Some rare source originally in the public library had been destroyed during the bombing and fires of World War II. My research work in Kiev was finished.

Our frequently-consulted tourist map of Kiev could soon be packed away, its borders covered with scrawled notes and its list of major tourist attractions duly checked off. The visit to the reconstructed nineteenth-century Ukrainian village had been frustrating, since the now familiar *Na remont* sign indicated that this too was under repair for a presumably indefinite period. We had to be content with the view from the locked gate about a half-mile above the village.

The hotel clerks had been able to make reservations for us at a unique riverbank restaurant. Nestled in a very attractive, park-like setting were individual, circular huts with thick clay walls, dazzlingly white in the hot July sunshine, but relatively cool inside under thatched roofs. A quick check at the reception desk on arrival confirmed our reservations. Dinner would be served, starting in about twenty minutes. Perhaps we would like to spend a few minutes strolling through the grounds? The roses were indeed lovely, the smiling receptionist agreed, as we walked out the door.

There were two tables inside our hut, though we were alone. A bright young waitress appeared with an impressive-looking menu. Knowing from previous experience that the actual selection available was much more limited, I asked doubtfully if they had all these items. The waitress seemed puzzled at the question, replying with an emphatic "Of course!" We scanned the three or four pages, asking occasionally about an interesting-sounding item only to be informed that, unfortunately, it was not available today.

What *did* they have? Patiently, she recited the various names under which Soviet restaurants list what is essentially a chunk of fried meat – *bifshtek*, *langette*, *kotlette*. But what could be more appropriate on this occasion than two orders of Chicken Kiev? Along with salad and vegetables they arrived in due course and were well worth waiting for – huge pieces of mature chicken breasts, de-boned, stuffed with butter and spices and deep-fried. As we cut into them, the buttery-garlicky mixture oozed out as it was supposed to, and they virtually melted in our mouths. Cups of tea and the celebrated Kiev Torte – recently franchised in far-off Japan, we were told – completed a meal approaching the levels of those served to us in friends' and relatives' homes.

A noisy group of Soviet citizens from somewhere in the Caucasus arrived, occupying the vacant table. "And what are you doing here?", the waitress asked rather abruptly, as she came in with our bill – under $10, incidentally.

"Waiting for you to serve us, of course," one of the men replied. "Bring us a menu, please!"

She retorted that she would neither serve them nor bring them a menu, but he insisted that they would sit there until she did. She stalked out of the door, returning in a few minutes with our change.

"So, you have come back to serve us after all," the would-be diner declared triumphantly.

"Definitely not," the waitress replied. "This place is not for the likes of you. It is reserved for government officials, economic administrators, top cultural personnel, and foreign tourists. And if you don't leave immediately I shall have to call the manager."

His earlier bantering tone gave way to anger. "Not for us ordinary, honest Soviet citizens, eh?" he snorted, banging the table as he got up to go. His friends arose and followed him to the door. "*I tak, ty nas vygan'aesh!*" (And so, you are driving us out!)

Smiling sweetly the waitress corrected him: "*Ia ne vygan'aiu – ia tol'ko otpravliaiu!*" (I am not driving you out – I am only seeing you off!)

They stormed out, eloquently cursing all waitresses, government officials, economic administrators, top cultural personnel, and especially – foreign tourists.

We stood for a long time taking our last look at the majestic Dnieper river. There, just below the bridge with its still-unrepaired rail through which the suicidal bus driver had crashed, hundreds of happy swimmers were splashing about or peacefully baking on golden sandy beaches. Somewhere in that dark east-bank forest was the Darnetskaia Baptist church, its bright and faithful witness consistently presenting Christ as the Light of the World. In that anonymous cluster of ugly apartment buildings, Pastor Kunets and his family daily demonstrated the unique beauty of a Christian home. Downstream, just around the bend, was the quiet bay where the baptismal service had taken place.

Petro had picked us up a couple of hours early on the day of the baptismal service, suggesting that we take an indirect route and thus be able to see more of the city. We drove along, stopping from time to time at some especially prominent vantage point to take in the panoramic view. From these points, the city of two million – boasting one of the world's highest proportions of greenery to overall urban area – gave the impression of a vast primeval forest. Here and there, like tiny islands on a green ocean, dull multi-storied office and apartment buildings looked down on the multi-coloured Byzantine domes of Orthodox churches.

But we also saw parts of Kiev not normally on tourists' itineraries. Attractive industrial districts are a rarity in any country, but even a quick drive past seemingly endless acres of run-down Soviet factories and adjacent slum-like housing can be particularly depressing. We wondered how many of the workers were anything like the beaming proletarians on the propaganda posters, shouting glory to the victorious Communist Party and joyfully fulfilling the current five-year plan goals.

Thanks to Petro's intimate knowledge of the city, beauty did overbalance ugliness. Attractive new buildings, with entire walls covered by artistically-excellent murals, relieved the sameness along many streets. The Baroque-style Mariinsky Palace and grounds were magnificent. And everywhere there were roses – in little oases dotting the concrete and cobblestones; in riotous banks of colour where majestic, tree-lined avenues ended in broad, sunlit squares; in veritable seas of scent and sight, pulsing throughout Kiev's public parks.

We arrived at the baptismal site early, joining a crowd of about four hundred. There were familiar faces from the three Union churches which we had visited. We also met fellow-believers from outlying points who had come to join in this service of witness. A cheerful wiry old Cossack, his magnificent moustache flaring out towards the shoulders of his gorgeously-embroidered Ukrainian shirt, assumed a typical serious look as he posed for a picture with me. Another visiting brother eyed our simple Japanese camera with what might be described as Christian envy. A business-like, balding forty-year-old man told us with a certain satisfaction of how an incoming collective farm manager had ousted him from his position.

"The newcomer managed to make a thorough mess of things. Now, local Party officials, faced with falling production and protests from mistreated workers, have been asking me – privately, of course – if I would be willing to replace him!", he concluded.

Church members and baptismal candidates had taken advantage of this special service to invite non-Christian friends and relatives. Of these, some were obviously sympathetic, others half-hostile. All of them were more than a little apprehensive about possible official opposition and repressive action, despite the fact that the participating churches had applied for and received official permission to hold the service. It would be one of four such baptismal services held by Kiev's four Union churches that year.

Attracted by the large crowd and full-throated singing by a veritable massed choir, curious boaters anchored their boats and watched the service. They heard a forceful presentation of the gospel, including urgent calls to repentance and faith in Christ. Explanation of the Biblical teaching on baptism was followed by a solemn charge to the candidates. They were reminded of the significance of this step of obedience, the increased Christian responsibilities which they were assuming, and the increased pressures which they would have to face. Dressed in white, one after another they walked out into the river, accompanied by two young men who were assisting the officiating pastors. There were fifty-six candidates who were immersed that day, thirty-five women and twenty-one men. Perhaps ten of them were over age thirty. Of these older ones, the most striking was a beaming octogenarian, who was literally carried out to the waiting pastor by the two assistants.

It had been a glorious service of witness, and the closing ceremony was especially moving. With joyful tears sparkling on their faces, the newly-baptized church members knelt in a circle on the grass, holding flowers presented to them by fellow-believers. The strong, clear voice of an officiating pastor broke through the animated conversation, calling us to the dedicatory prayer.

Scattered groups broke up, their members hurrying to form a living ring of love around those kneeling on the grass. Lil and I took our places on either side of Pastor Kunets from the Darnetskaia church. With arms uplifted, Iakov Dukhonchenko, senior presbyter for the Ukraine, led in a glorious prayer of dedication and praise. For an illuminating moment, past and present, Kiev Christians and Canadian Christians, were fused into one. In a very profound sense, we were discovering our roots, and the roots of that astonishing spiritual strength, demonstrated so powerfully in the lives of our Ukrainian grandparents.

"And when did you say you plan to leave us?" asked Pastor Kunets as we made our way back to where Petro had parked his car. With one foot in heaven after the experiences of the last three hours, we were tempted to reply that we had no intention of leaving at all. He jotted down the time of our departure, promising to be at the railway station with his two oldest children to see us off. Petro would be picking us up at the hotel.

Checking out was accomplished with only minor confusion over costs. Articles of clothing and gifts from Canada had been distributed to believers in the three cities and in Borodianka village, but our suitcases were becoming almost circular. An appreciative desk clerk had gratefully accepted the decorated kerchief which we had bought for her in the foreign currency shop. But she had insisted that we accept a beautiful piece of traditional Ukrainian embroidery in return. Our last-night visit with Petro, Anna, and their children had been delightful, including the tape recording of their individual greetings to Uncle Stepan and his family in Canada. But they also gave us several gifts for Uncle Stepan and his family, together with several others for ourselves. The large Sony tape recorder-radio, purchased in Moscow for Anton in Leningrad, would be greatly appreciated as a tool for taping short-wave Christian broadcasts. Knowledge of that appreciation helped to compensate for the machine's weight and the space it took.

Strained beyond its tested strength, the lock of one suitcase broke as Petro was lugging it into the railway station. A hurried search through his little Zaporozhets uncovered a length of stout cord which at least would keep the bulging sides from parting company. Repairs made, we moved along the platform, searching for the proper car.

Pastor Kunets and his children, an attractive blonde seventeen year-old and her handsome older brother, were standing there already. Suddenly, an anguished-looking young woman rushed up to us, declaring piteously that there had been a sudden illness in the family; she had to get home to her stricken mother immediately, and she was unable to pay the twenty-ruble fare.

Taken aback, and, as it turned out, almost taken in, I was about to respond to her seemingly genuine plight. Petro's meaningful shake of the head stopped me. Not unkindly, he suggested to the suddenly-calm young woman that she should consult with the station officials. As she walked off, he explained the two contradictory stages of the incident.

"She is not the only one who comes up to prosperous-looking travellers with touching appeals for help. She'll probably pick up quite a bit of money today," he concluded.

We entered our compartment, carrying an armful of blood-red roses, a farewell gift from Pastor Kunet's daughter. She stood there with her father and brother, all three of them waving to us and smiling. We gestured toward ourselves, urging them to accompany us. Shaking their heads and still beaming, they returned the gesture, inviting us to stay in Kiev. Unable to hear one another because of the increasing engine noise, we nevertheless saw and returned their final *Do svedanyes* – part promise and part benediction.

"I'm so glad you are sharing our compartment," our fellow-traveller said as the train pulled out of the station. "You saw that bunch of Negroes that got on the train? Foreign students – why do they have to come here anyway? I was horrified to think that some of them might end up in my compartment. Then, I'd have to endure their terrible music and their equally terrible smell all the way to Leningrad!"

22: *Last Days in Leningrad*

Twenty-three weary hours later the train pulled into the Leningrad station. Hopefully, we would be able to meet Anton and Vera at their apartment, as planned, since we did not know the way to their church. The cab dropped us off at the familiar Oktiabrskaia Hotel, where a smiling registration clerk promptly informed us that the university had, of course, made all the arrangements. Presumably there had been no complaint about their having to pay for the TV and refrigerator on our first visit. In a few minutes we were in our old room, soaking the weariness away in a large tubful of hot water.

Refreshed, and dabbed semi-dry with the familiar tea-towel-like bath towels, we struggled into our clothes and ran toward the subway station. Crowds of Sunday-morning picnickers, carrying large lunchbaskets, jostled against one another.

"Why don't you watch your feet!", barked an angry woman to an apologetic one behind her, who had accidentally stepped on the heel of the indignant one's sandal. "Now what am I going to do – get you to buy me another one?" she sputtered, waving her badly-ripped, plastic sandal in the offender's face.

Another passenger looked nervously about her. Carefully lifting the lid of her lunch basket she began whispering into it. Intrigued, Lil leaned across the back of the seat as the woman continued her whispering. "You're not supposed to be here, you know. We could get into a lot of trouble if an official spotted you. So be very quiet and I'll give you something very nice when we get home," she promised, closing the lid. A barely audible meow indicated that the basket's occupant understood the need for discretion.

Anton had already left with the car, but Vera had stayed at home, assuming that we might possibly be a bit late. We left the large, long-transported Sony tape-recorder and a few gifts which we had brought, and walked quickly toward the nearby railway station for the short ride to the church. Familiar faces beamed smiles of welcome as we entered the crowded room. An exchange of gestures, an affirmative nod, and the dear old pastor was announcing that Brother Nesdoly would bring us a few words.

The wide-eyed little children still chuckled politely behind their hands. Young people who had sung so harmoniously, accompanying themselves with various stringed instruments, gazed steadily at the preacher who was also a professor. Parents from their mid-twenties to their mid-forties listened attentively, nodding in approval and offering helpful suggestions when my somewhat improved Russian language skills broke down in the search for the right expression.

Though far from home, the scene was profoundly home-like. Together, the different age groups in the little Russian Baptist assembly that morning, represented a living picture of forty years of my own life. And, if the next forty years of life's experiences should produce in me a Christian character approaching that of the saintly old pastor sitting beside me – *Slava Bogu*! (Glory to God!)

"Well, did you pick a restaurant where we can take you out for dinner?" we asked as we chugged along in the valiant little Zaporozhets.

"Yes, we certainly have," Anton replied gravely. We waited for one of them to add the name of the restaurant.

"– – – –," said Vera simply, giving their home address. Having once previously offered to take them to the Hotel Astoria and been told kindly that "it would be best for all of us if we were not seen there with you," we understood.

After the simple meal, we settled down to share experiences. Young Alyosha was delighted that we had managed to find a few additional packages of American gum and even more delighted to be able to experiment with the magnificent Sony tape-recorder-radio. His father chuckled appreciatively as we described the attempts of the two Armenian entrepreneurs to buy the machine from us.

"Yes," he agreed, "they could sell it for at least a thousand rubles in Erevan."

Lil's account of her encounter with the Kremlin officials' chauffeur – and a suggestion that there might one day be saints in the Soviet Caesar's household, was received with fervent *Slava Bogu's*.

"There's a rumour going around that Kosygin's wife is a believer," Vera commented.

"There's also that joke about the identification contest," Anton chuckled. "It's in the form of a poem, including these lines: (My "free" translation)

> 'Who has eyebrows black and bushy,
> Who has got a job so cushy?' "

"Yes," laughed Vera, "and then the last two lines go like this:

> 'Give us an answer – do, my dears
> And we'll give to you – ten years!' "

We mentioned our Bible studies with officers from the various embassies and the problem of listening devices seeming to be everywhere. "Well, to speak frankly,"

Anton commented, "I can't be sure that the one device which I found in this apartment is the only one." Both of them nodded in enthusiastic agreement as we told them of how we had read the Scripture and prayed rather loudly and especially distinctly, hoping that any listener would literally "get the message."

"Of course," I interjected, "there are some other ways in which you can get those listening devices to work for you." Briefly, we recounted Marion's experiences with the banana problem in the diplomatic grocery store.

"A whole kilo of bananas," young Alyosha sighed.

Vera gave her eleven year-old son a consoling hug, explaining to us that he had had a banana once and enjoyed it tremendously. Now he would like to have another one sometime, but they had never been able to find bananas in their grocery stores.

Anton already knew about the problems being experienced by the church in Rostov, quite apart from the police break-up of the planned young people's rally two months previously. "But," he added, brightening, "I heard of a remarkable incident which occurred during the Khar'kov rally. A young woman, who had been standing at the meeting for hours, tears running down her cheeks, was asked what was troubling her.

" 'I was here earlier,' she said, 'but I could not bear it; so, I left. I went to the station, purchased a ticket, and got on the train, just to get away from the service. But after having gone through several stops I simply could not go on – something was drawing me back. I was in terrible distress and so I returned to the service. Now here I am. I cannot stop crying. I am a helpless sinner.'

"And so," Anton continued, "she told the story of her dissolute life. She had truly gone to the very bottom. Those listening were deeply touched. But then," – and the words came tumbling out – "they all rejoiced together as they saw, once again, how God finds lost souls and returns them to Himself."

We told them of Lil's experiences with Elizaveta and the umbrellas in the foreign currency shop and of the wonderful fellowship enjoyed with the young girl and her mother in their suburban Moscow apartment. All the while, seventeen-year-old Inessa had been listening impassively. Now, with a languid yawn, she got up and moved to her bedroom with its walls covered with pages torn from glossy Western magazines. Vera sighed deeply, her eyes on the closing door.

We sat in silence for a few minutes. "I'm going to make some more tea," Vera announced, moving into the kitchen. I glanced idly at the familiar bookcase, noticing a thick stack of about two hundred pages of paper.

"You haven't seen that yet," said Anton. "Take a look at it and see how we are managing to do some printing."

It turned out to be a fairly detailed syllabus of a basic pastoral training course, beautifully hand-written and duplicated on an old-fashioned hectograph. Another new item in the bookcase was a boxful of very attractive Christian greeting cards, produced by silkscreen printing.

"It's certainly not easy," Anton observed as Vera refilled his cup. "As you know, private ownership of duplicating equipment is not permitted in our country. Buying large quantities of paper can only be done without arousing suspicions if a number of us buy a small package each, at several shops, over several days.

"But here's something that will help speed up our printing," he said, opening one of the copies of *Bratskii Listok* (*Brotherly Leaflet*) which were stacked in the bookcase. Along with a brief notice of a recent government discovery and shutdown of a hidden Christian printing press, there was a neat sketch of a proposed replacement. "It will be harder for them to discover this time," Anton declared, "because this press will be small enough to fit in a couple of suitcases, and none of those involved in the printing process will know who the others are. And," he concluded with a happy grin, "a recent test run indicates that this machine should be able to print four hundred New Testaments a day."

The afternoon had passed quickly. We would be leaving for Helsinki tomorrow morning. "Well," said Anton heartily, "we'll take you on a farewell tour of our beautiful Leningrad on our way to the Poklonaia Gora church. After all, I was at one time a taxi driver."

Heedless of possible car-sickness, we squeezed into the little vehicle. After her usual protesting growls, coughs, and belch of smoke she settled down to a steady dull roar as we drove through the streets of Leningrad.

There was the huge St. Isaac's cathedral, the Christian inscriptions over its massive doors continuing their mute testimony in an atheist land. Across the river from the equestrian statue of the city's founder, Peter the Great, were the university and the Academy of Sciences. Further downstream on Vasilevskii Island was the site of the *Dom Evangeliia* (House of the Gospel). Now a factory, it had once been the 2,000-seat meeting place of St. Petersburg's first Baptist church, founded by the dynamic William Fetler.

"And somewhere around here," Anton observed as we neared the massive Winter Palace, "probably in Palace Square near the Alexander I column with its angel-and-cross top, there was apparently a mass demonstration a few days ago. According to reports which I heard, there were about two thousand people there, shouting liberal slogans, making protest speeches, and so forth. One man shouted out that he knew he would get ten years for what he was doing, but he would at least have ten minutes to say what he really wanted to say. And that's about all he did have," Anton concluded, "because the police were there in full force very soon to break up the demonstration and make mass arrests."

As we crossed the nearby bridge, he recalled an incident from his taxi-driving career. His passenger, a visitor to Leningrad, had at first asked for a similar cultural-historical tour. Quickly tiring of that, he had asked Anton with a leer to tell him the location of the best prostitutes in the city.

" 'I know nothing about that,' I told him politely." Anton continued, turning around unnervingly to be better heard by us back-seat passengers. " 'Now, if you had asked me to tell you what you must know about God and Jesus Christ, I could readily oblige.' Well, he was so ashamed, yet so interested, that he listened to the Gospel for almost an hour as we drove around. And he gladly took the Christian literature which I offered him."

We rumbled on through industrial and residential districts on our way to church. Anton and Vera shared with us their desire to emigrate, adding that they had applied for permission to do so. Yes, they agreed, both of them had an important ministry in the USSR. Vera smiled lovingly as we assured them that Anton had talents, boldness, and zeal which enabled him to do what few other Christian leaders could do.

We knew, of course, that material advantage was not their motive for wanting to emigrate. Freedom, especially the freedom to worship and evangelize, is indeed a precious thing, we agreed. Unfortunately, so many Western Christians take that freedom for granted, failing to make use of their privileges and opportunities, and neglecting the spiritual aspect of life. If, despite all these considerations, Anton and Vera were both convinced that it was God's will for them to emigrate, He would certainly over-ride any obstacles which the Soviet authorities could impose. We would both pray for them and consult Canadian government authorities to see what could be done to help.

We were warmly welcomed on the occasion of our second homecoming to Poklonaia Gora. Our beloved Manya was there in her usual spot, her radiantly happy face lighting up with an extra glow as she came over to embrace her 'returned children.' Once again, we were ushered on to the platform by one of the preaching brethren as the service began. In a moment Lil gave me a little nudge, gesturing toward the balcony at the back of the church. There, making his way quickly up the stairs, was the young Canadian engineer, Michael, whom we had met in Kiev.

At the end of the service we made our way quickly to the back of the church, nodding to various acquaintances as we moved through the crowd. Anton and Vera were already there when we joined Michael and a strikingly-attractive dark-haired girl. He introduced her to us as Tamara, a Leningrader whom he had first met in Nairobi, when she was there on an exchange program between Kenya and the USSR. Introductions over, Anton immediately asked the two young people what they had thought of the service.

"Very familiar, from my boyhood," Michael replied in an interesting mixture of Ukrainian and English, "but the choirs I remember were certainly not anything like as good as the one I heard tonight."

Tamara was politely appreciative, speaking of the experience as "very interesting." A native of Leningrad, she had, of course, known about the Baptist church, but this was the first time she had attended a service.

"I'm Jewish," she replied in response to Anton's question about her faith, "but only by birth and tradition. As a matter of fact," she laughed, "the last time I was in a synagogue was some years ago in Nairobi."

"Well friends," said Anton and Vera in chorus, "you must all come over to our place for tea."

Michael seemed quite willing; the girl replied with a non-committal, "Thank you for the invitation" as she noted the address. Lil and I drove off with Anton and Vera. Michael suggested that he and Tamara would come along later, by bus and subway.

We had previously informed Anton and Vera about Michael's background and the possibility of his being at the service tonight. "God's ways are indeed past finding out," I observed as we bounced along. "Here Lil and I are from Nova Scotia. Visiting Kiev we meet a mother from Saskatchewan and her son from Nairobi. That son comes to Leningrad to attend the first church service he has been to in years, and he brings along his Jewish girl friend to the first Christian service which she has ever attended. And now the two of them are coming to visit a Leningrad Baptist preacher in his home."

It was a pleasantly warm evening and so we decided to wait outside, looking from time to time toward the nearby subway stop. Within the hour Michael and Tamara emerged on the sidewalk, talking animatedly. Almost before we could catch their attention she had returned to the underground platform and Michael came over slowly by himself. He explained quickly to us – in English – that his girl friend was a little bit afraid to come. "According to her," he explained, "some overly-zealous Baptist witnessers had been giving her mother a rather hard time." We translated for Anton and Vera.

Warmly hospitable, but getting right to the most important thing in life, Anton looked steadily into Michael's eyes. "Well, my dear young friend," he said gently but urgently, "is it not time that you repented of your sin and returned to the faith of your Christian parents?"

More than a little taken aback by this very direct approach, Michael was at a loss for words, whether half-forgotten Ukrainian ones or his usually fluent English ones. Looking helplessly at us he muttered: "Hey! Tell him to take it easy!"

Anton had once told us that his years of experience in witnessing to people from all walks of life had taught him several lessons. One of the most important was that unbelievers are not impressed with a Christian's ability to give a rational defence of Christianity. It is rather genuine Christian concern and love, clearly demonstrated, that wins the heart. During the next two hours we had a humbling demonstration of how well Anton and Vera had learned that lesson.

They spoke simply and specifically from their personal experience, of the tragic moral and spiritual effects of atheism in the USSR. They spoke with even deeper feeling of a Christian parent's broken-heartedness over a child's sinful rebellion, not only against all that those parents held most dear, but especially against God. Was it not the wonder of wonders, that for sinful man, a Hell-bound and Hell-deserving rebel, our God gave His only Son, "that whosoever believeth in Him, should not perish, but have everlasting life!"

Interspersed with other topics, the conversation persistently and perfectly naturally kept coming back to the spiritual dimension. Initially very much on guard, Michael soon relaxed, speaking very frankly about his disgust with those who merely professed to be followers of Christ, but his admiration for genuine Christ-likeness. He shared his doubts, born of shrewd observation and prolonged exposure to non-Christian societies, about Christianity's exclusive claims.

I could think of all sorts of Christian apologetics responses, but decided to continue to play the more passive role of two-way translator. Anton never bothered to argue with him. Quoting extensively from the Scriptures, unfailingly warm and gracious in manner, Anton kept going back to basic, personal questions. "But how will *you* answer for your own sins before a perfectly holy God? And what will *you* do with the Lord Jesus Christ?"

It was time to leave. Michael bowed his head with the rest of us as Anton offered a stirring prayer of benediction, but one which included a concise statement of the gospel message. Little Alyosha smiled manfully, but blinked several times. Inessa listened thoughtfully as Lil told her: "I really look forward to hearing – and very soon – that you have turned your life over to Jesus Christ." Smiling hopefully, Anton and Vera nodded their emphatic agreement.

Could it be that all the things we had shared with these two new friends could have happened during about eight days, spread over a month-long period? "Well," they laughed through their tears, "maybe the next time we meet we'll be drinking tea with you in Canada!" It was the emotional equivalent of being released from Anton's crushing farewell bear hug. And, to mention an additional small mercy, he did not insist on driving us back to our hotel.

Despite the exhaustion of that very full day and the immediately-previous day-long railway journey, we did not sleep very much on our last night in the USSR. Our luggage was packed and the checking-out formalities concluded long before the promised taxi arrived to take us to the airport. After standing in the wrong queue for half an hour or so, we were directed to a special desk where the clerk quickly verified our tickets. Then it was time for the customs ordeal.

Our original declarations on our foreign currency were checked against receipts for exchange into rubles and our extra rubles converted into American dollars. So far so good! A sharp-eyed officer looked slowly back and forth at our row of three suitcases and then asked us to open the little one. His quick search revealed nothing out of the ordinary and the suitcases were duly sent out to the waiting Finnair jet. Only one more checkpoint remained – the passport examination. Beyond that was the freedom of the waiting room.

These men are a special breed in a land where officials generally inspire varying degrees of anxiety. Presumably, face-to-face interrogation by a KGB officer would be worse. But we had never experienced anything quite like the impact of watching one of these officers check our tickets, going over every word, it seemed, with microscopic carefulness. Then, after what seemed to be a very long time, the tickets were handed back and a curt request for passports began the process all over again. Only this time the tension was much greater, as the officer stared searchingly into our faces, looked at the passport pictures just as searchingly, and then looked at our faces again. As if this were not enough, he added a mysterious look at something or another under the counter as he repeated his original two-point check with this three-dimensional scrutiny. Like gimlets, his cold eyes bored relentlessly through those of his intended victims, seeking to discover what was hidden in the furthest recesses of one's mind.

A frustrated-sounding double thump and our stamped passports were shoved back across the counter. We stepped through the doorway, feeling as if a huge stone had been suddenly lifted from our backs. In seconds we were talking and laughing with other, similarly-relieved outbound passengers. It was hard to remind ourselves that we had not yet left the USSR.

The Finnair jet was like a familiar oasis. Even before take-off air-conditioned coolness and ice-cold orange juice provided welcome relief from the airport's stuffiness and the July heat. Everything was so incredibly clean, and everything – even the toilets – smelled so incredibly fresh. The three blonde stewardesses looked absolutely stunning in their up-to-the-minute uniforms. And everybody was smiling.

Forty-five minutes later we landed at Helsinki's International airport. Smiling customs officers cleared us through at the rate of about twenty seconds per traveller. A smiling clerk at the currency exchange handed over the correct amount in Finnish marks almost before I had signed the travellers' cheque. Within minutes the motherly-looking woman at the accommodations desk had us booked into an economy hotel. We left the bright airport building with its freshly-waxed floors and sparkling windows in a tearful daze.

The spotless, glass-walled bus whisked us along a smooth freeway toward the city, hundreds of early-afternoon drivers whizzing by. It was not yet home, but it was all very much like home. Even the rapidly-recurring gas stations had us pointing delightedly.

The elevator worked smoothly and did not smell of urine. The room was large, bright and attractively-decorated. The bathroom gleamed and the towels were thick. And it all cost about one-third the price of our room in nearby Leningrad.

We walked downtown. There were no queues, and the clerks smiled obligingly as I showed Lil through the department stores where I had shopped during my 1971 research trip. The farmers' and fisherman's stalls by the waterfront were just as overflowing as I had remembered them.

We manouvered through the friendly crowds. Suddenly we stopped, looking at one another in silent sorrow. After a careful examination of the vendor's overflowing table, Lil and I each selected one item. Looking across the Gulf of Finland we slowly ate the delicious bananas and thought of a wistful eleven-year-old boy in Leningrad, a mere forty-five minutes away by air.

Epilogue (1985)

"The more things change, the more they remain the same."

In the words of the writer of Ecclesiastes, "Let us hear the conclusion of the whole matter." To what extent does the overall picture of Soviet evangelicals presented in this book still hold true?

The general features of the Soviet system in which they must live and work remain much the same. Changes in political leadership from Brezhnev to Gorbachev have not been accompanied by any significant change in the reality of Communist Party dictatorship and ultimate control over all aspects of life. The economic system, faced with increasing demands from its capital investment, military, and consumer sectors has grown very slowly. According to one American economist the main Soviet economic issue of the 1980s will be the problem of adapting to stringency. Continuing shortages and quality problems in consumer goods and services have resulted, in the words of one of our correspondents, in "longer queues and shorter tempers." It remains to be seen whether the tightening of discipline and the crackdown on corruption and alcoholism, begun under Andropov and accentuated by Gorbachev, will be able to solve some of the basic problems.

This tightening of economic discipline has been part of a more general trend toward stricter enforcement of existing laws and establishment of some more restrictive new ones. (An example is recent legislation restricting citizens' contacts with tourists and imposing stiff fines on offenders.) While the negative implications are obvious, there have been some positive aspects to this development. It can mean, for example, some lessening of the serious problem of arbitrary action by government officials. It has also meant increased – if perhaps only temporary – security for those individuals or groups prepared to play strictly by the rules. On the other hand, one must remember that "socialist legality" as practised in the USSR lacks some of the guarantees of legality which exist in the West. Chief among these would be an independent judiciary (including independent defence lawyers), a genuine political opposition and a free media to act as a check on political-judicial arbitrariness. The efficiency of Soviet justice can be judged from the fact that, according to studies done by the US State Department and Amnesty International, during the Soviet era no one brought to trial for political or religious-law offences has ever been acquitted.

Broadly speaking, for the Soviet evangelicals "socialist legality" has meant two very different things. The Union leadership and churches, generally willing to play by the rules, and favoured – for its own divide-and-rule reasons – by the régime, have been given considerable freedom. Back and forth visits with co-religionists in the West have provided moral and material support, learning experiences, and increased opportunities to preach the gospel. Though neither uncontroversial nor an unmixed blessing, Billy Graham's 1982 and 1984 visits can be seen in this light, as can Soviet Baptists' participation in the activities of the Baptist World Alliance. Some tens of thousands of copies of the Scriptures have been legally sent to the USSR by Western Bible Societies.

Internally, freedom within the framework of "socialist

legality" has meant some increased opportunities to publish, to build, to teach and to preach. Regular legal printings of hymnals and the Scriptures, added to permitted imports and unofficial "gifts" from abroad, have helped to alleviate the scarcity of Christian literature. The Poklonaia Gora church in Leningrad, for example, apparently enjoys a 95% personal possession rate for copies of the Scriptures among its members. Of course, more remote churches are not so favoured.

That same church has recently completed major renovation which has doubled its previous seating capacity. Among many other centres, Minsk Baptists have a very large new building, and according to Union reports, some 45 new churches were opened in southern Siberia during the period 1979–1984.

Church growth continues (admitted even in Soviet sources), as can be seen in crowded services, establishment of 7 "daughter churches" in Leningrad's suburbs, and waiting lists for church and choir membership. An especially encouraging development has been the steady influx of young people, reflecting in part the impact of the so-called "religious renaissance" in the USSR. A Soviet investigator was startled to discover, for example, that a relatively small Baptist congregation in Central Asia had some 60–70 young people actively involved. According to the Union's senior presbyter for the North-west district, the number of young people in the churches has increased five-fold from 1977–1984. Some young pastors in the district themselves heard the gospel for the first time as recently as six years ago.

The churches continue to hold their regular services of worship, instruction, and evangelism – as often as six times per week, in many cases. In fact, the Leningrad church seems to have added some meetings since our visit in 1978. There is a regular Monday evening Bible study and an informal Wednesday evening evangelistic outreach to which the members regularly invite friends who are unbelievers. In all of these, young people are playing an increasingly important role.

This rapid growth of the youth component has been accompanied by some growing pains and generational perspective problems. Perhaps the most dramatic example of this has been the emergence of the so-called Christian rock group "The Trumpet Call", led by a Leningrad Baptist, Valeri Barinov. Disagreements over the music itself and Barinov's ministry to the drop-outs of Soviet society, together with his conflict with the authorities, eventually led to his expulsion from the church and his arrest in March, 1984.

For the Reformers, "socialist legality" over the past six years has been experienced in the form of increased repression. In part, this is because of their refusal to play by the rules, particularly as they apply to registration and what they see as its opportunities for unacceptable régime meddling in internal church matters. More specifically, aspects of state-imposed laws judged to be justifiably disobeyable include the restrictions on publication, evangelism, Christian charitable activity, and Christian education of children.

In part, the Reformers have fallen victim to the critics' crackdown on the general dissident movement, which began in the late 1970s and had virtually destroyed that movement by the early 1980s. Assuming that its most radical and most vocal critics were also the most dangerous, the régime struck at them first. Thus, for the Reformers as well, the mid-1970s relaxation soon gave way to renewed harrassment, complete with the familiar house searches and interrogation, fines, physical abuse, arrests, and imprisonment. The approximately 40 prisoners of conscience in 1978 have increased to over 200 by

1985. A new feature of this repression campaign has been the phenomenon of re-sentencing of these prisoners for additional terms of up to five years – sometimes even before the original term was up. This power has been given to prison and camp authorities by recent (1983) amendments to the criminal code.

But these repressive measures have neither silenced the Reformers nor stopped their religious activity. They have continued to hold both open and secret worship services, conduct aggressive evangelism and an amazingly effective Christian education programme, and support the families of imprisoned breadwinners. Apart from an undetermined amount of aid received unofficially from sources within and outside the USSR, they are managing to do all this on their own. Of special importance in sustaining Reform activity – even more so than in the case of Union churches – is the role of the Christian family.

Though members of Union churches have been relatively unmolested, given past and contemporary experience, the atheist régime's unchanging goals, and the precarious nature of "socialist legality", one wonders if the Union leadership's optimism and confidence is very well-grounded. (According to one specialist, that confidence is reflected in the leadership's planning on a five-year basis.) One can also question the official Soviet and Union leadership view that the Reformers are not being persecuted for their religious beliefs, but simply for violating Soviet criminal law. At best that explanation is inadequate; at worst it is unjust and dishonest.

At the official level, the quarter-century Union-Reform conflict continues, perhaps with even some additional sharpness. Factors contributing to this development include the régime's uneven treatment of the two groups, the Union leadership's stance toward both the régime and the Reformers, and the Reformers' heroic/foolhardy, persistent refusal to change their principled/fanatical ideas and methods. An additional international dimension has been added to the conflict since 1979, when Reform leader Georgi Vins and his family left the USSR. Vins became head of the Reformers' International Representation body, publicizing the Reform cause, organizing counter-sessions at the Toronto congress of the Baptist World Alliance, and being supported by, among others, a number of West German Baptist churches established by Germans who had emigrated from the USSR since the late 1970s.

Vins' estimate (1981) that the Reform membership is around 100,000, not including children, has been considered by some specialists to be inflated. Age, imprisonment and exile have taken a heavy toll on Reform leadership. Many have simply grown weary in or of the prolonged struggle against both régime and Union. Individuals and churches have defected from the Reformers' Council of Churches. Some have returned to the Union fold. Others have joined Independent churches. (Over 300 congregations, at last count, have been permitted to register as Independents.)

Leading Western specialists have drawn completely opposite conclusions about the overall situation and prospects of the Soviet evangelicals. Optimists generally focus on the Union, pessimists on the Reformers. Still unexamined, for the most part, are questions relating to some possible implications of the Union's success. One should remember, for example, that the Reformers' original protests were against both the Union's undue co-operation with the régime and against worldliness in the Union churches. A weakened Reform influence, therefore, can mean less overall resistance to régime pressures and to those forces working against the maintenance of stringent membership requirements.

Three features of the contemporary situation seem to have particular relevance for this matter. First, various long-range developments and the present relatively-privileged status of the Union churches are combining to produce a leadership which is, in some senses, less "separate" from Soviet society generally. Secondly, the Union leadership's frequent contacts with the West and their sometimes overly-uncritical admiration for Western evangelicalism, together with a kind of general cultural "Westernization" of Soviet youth could make for future problems. Finally, the measure of relative freedom and social acceptance which the Union churches enjoy is not without its dangers. In this connection, one specialist has noted that the East German government is presently experimenting with a new policy on religion, which has been borrowed from the West. By giving the churches more freedom and socio-economic privileges, the East German authorities expect to witness the self-destruction of those same churches.

Ultimately, of course, the future of Soviet evangelicalism is in the hands of the One who began the good work over one hundred years ago and will undoubtedly complete it until the day of Christ. Surely, whether the opposition comes as a roaring lion or as a fake angel of light, Christ will build His church, and the gates of Hell shall not prevail against it.

Since God does work through human instruments and since these Soviet evangelicals are also part of the body of Christ, how can we in the West help them? First, we need to be better-informed about that complex community, both for our own benefit and for more effective publicizing. Secondly, written communication with believers and the even more valuable personal visits to the churches in the USSR serve as a great encouragement to the believers and a challenge to one's own spiritual standards.

Publicity of various kinds can also help to protect the believers from more severe repressive measures. The same can be said for sending petitions to Soviet authorities on behalf of persecuted believers. These must be factually accurate and respectful, rather than belligerent in tone.

One should investigate very carefully before supporting financially or otherwise any of the approximately 200 Western agencies that have some form of ministry to the Christians in the USSR. Are they doctrinally sound? Is their focus truly spiritual, rather than political? Do they pass the test of basic integrity in such matters as sound knowledge and accurate reporting, financial honesty, and avoidance of undue expenditure on administration?

Short-wave Christian radio broadcasts from the West, presently totalling over 200 hours per week, are undoubtedly the best means available to help Soviet believers and reach unbelievers. Where training and literature shortages limit the teaching ministry of the local church, radio can provide a supplement. For believers in areas remote from any local church, radio broadcasts provide virtually the only spiritual food to be had. According to a recent study, perhaps as many as 80% of new converts were initially attracted to Christianity through hearing the gospel on radio. Scattered throughout the USSR today, according to one informed estimate, are some 39,000 "radio churches".

The Soviet evangelicals themselves gave these same suggestions when we asked them how we could help them. Yet our question was more frequently answered by another suggestion. It was always the same, whether the respondent came from a rural or an urban area, from a Union, Reform, or Independent church, from whatever age group, educational or ethnic background. It came in the form of a single word:

Pray!